The Cockburn Line

By Lionel Noble
Edited by Jeff Noble

The Cockburn Line
By Lionel Noble
Edited by Jeff Noble

Published in 2025 in South Australia by Staurolite Books
Copyright © 1995 and 2025 by Lionel Noble

All rights reserved. Other than for the purposes and subject to the conditions prescribed under the *Copyright Act,* no part of this publication may be reproduced, stored in a retrieval system or transmitted in any form or by any means, electronic, mechanical, photocopying, recording or otherwise, without the prior permission of the publisher.

This work includes historical photographs. Every effort has been made to trace copyright holders and obtain necessary permissions. If any material has been used inadvertently without appropriate acknowledgement, the publisher welcomes contact to rectify the oversight in future editions.

Print ISBN: 978-1-7641335-3-1

All content is original. AI has been used for editing purposes only.

Maps used with permission of National Library of Australia.
SA Chief Engineer for Railways & Vaughan, A. & South Australia Surveyor-General's Office, *Map shewing lines of railways in South Australia, Novr. 1910* , object 234151847

Cover design : Jeff Noble
Cover image: Peterborough Division T-class locomotive 199 by Lionel Noble

 A catalogue record for this book is available from the National Library of Australia

https://staurolitebooks.com.au
Copies of the book can be ordered through
https://lionelnoble.com

Dedication

To the dedicated engine crews and railway staff who, over many decades, faithfully maintained and operated the Cockburn narrow-gauge line for the South Australian Railways.

Preface

It was in my senior years, while living in Peterborough, that I began to organise fragments of history relating to the Peterborough Division of the South Australian Railways (SAR). My two sons, Jeff and Mark, showed interest and it was due to their enthusiasm and encouragement that this history has been collated. This book is a record of things as I remember them, along with the memories of senior railway people and others, many of whom are no longer with us.

I've heard many stories in passing, usually beginning with 'I remember one time …' While many of these tales recount the hard times on the line—difficult locomotives and conditions, bad water, dust storms, floods and breakdowns—they were always laced with humour. So many stories were never recorded and so are lost. This book is my humble effort to keep some of those stories alive.

When I was a young married man, local photographer Les Rasmus from Hurlstone Street in Peterborough encouraged my interest in photography. He didn't just take pictures but also shared captivating stories from his youth at Ucolta, and it was that, perhaps more than anything, which inspired me to explore the past.

Lionel Noble, 1995
https://lionelnoble.com

Editor's Preface

The Cockburn Line offers a firsthand account of a bygone railway era. This book chronicles my father's experiences and recollections from his working life on the narrow gauge Peterborough Division of the South Australian Railways (SAR), specifically, the section stretching between Peterborough and Cockburn on the New South Wales border. His story spans from the latter years of World War II through to the line's closure in 1970, capturing both the routine and memorable moments of life on the rails. In its heyday, this line (and its extension to Port Pirie) was one of the busiest in Australia.

This book was originally written by Dad for his children—my sister Meryn, brother Mark and myself. He gave each of us a bound copy, and I assume only a small number of other copies were made. Seeing the historical importance of his work for those interested in the narrow-gauge steam era, I decided to edit and publish the book.

This is not a chronological record, but is structured around each station on the line and it's respective section of track. It begins with a description of the Peterborough yard and its workings, and then moves progressively up the line. Many of the stations mentioned no longer exist. Dad's original edition had detailed information perhaps only appreciated by avid railway enthusiasts. Much of that detail has not been included in this edition, but all the stories he told have been retained.

Dad's descriptions of places, events and people were familiar to me as I was born in the early 1950s when the line was still busy. What impressed me was the strong bond among the men, their passion for their job, the fun they had and how they supported each other. This unity wasn't just a quirk of that era;

the difficult conditions and risks on the Cockburn Line brought out the best in them. Editing the book was bittersweet because it made me realise how much had been lost to progress.

My hope is that this record of Dad's memories will give insight into the bygone world of the railway men of the Cockburn Line on the Peterborough Division of the South Australian Railways. Further information can be found in Dad's extensive photographic collection at https://lionelnoble.com, where I can also be reached via the contact form.

Jeff Noble, 2025
https://lionelnoble.com

Acknowledgements

My heartfelt thanks go to the following people:

Les Rasmus for permitting me to copy many of his photographs, some of which now appear in this book.

Alex Grunbach (NSW), friend, historian and author; thank you for the various details you shared with me over the years.

Mrs Eileen Smith (100 years old in 1994) for her contribution regarding the township of Cockburn, her birthplace.

To everyone who over the years supplied details about the Cockburn Line: Ken Sleep, Tim Jenkins, Joe "Paddy" Harding, Archie Williams, George "Catta" Miller, Gordon "Gonga" Wight, Harold Mesecke, Martin, Dan and Jack Brennan, Jack O'Dea, W Meadows, Chris O'Dea, Harry Hanlon, Jim Ritchie, Bert Bradtberg and others. These were the main storytellers, sadly all now deceased.

To others who assisted in numerous ways: Alan Welsby, Peter Moroney, Ray Schell, Merv Yates, Jim McKeough, Arthur Creeper, Peter Smallacombe, Ken Moody, Les Cook, Nancy and Stan Andrews, Fay Shermer (née Finlay), Dulcie Freeman, Heine Weich and George Bishop.

To my sons, Jeff and Mark, for their encouragement; for Jeff's wife Wendy for placing everything on computer and editing what I had written; and to Mark for his artwork in setting the original manuscript and photographs.

Finally, my wife, Lorace, for putting up with all my chasing after photographs and stories and for tolerating a room full of historical material which she refers to as "junk"!

My thanks to everyone who contributed to this simple record of the Cockburn Line.

Lionel Noble, 1995

Explanatory Notes

Throughout the book you'll find frequent references to "up" and "down" movements. A "down" movement was a train travelling *from Peterborough*, while an "up" movement was one travelling *toward Peterborough*.

Imperial measurements have been retained for consistency with the Cockburn Line's operational history, with metric equivalents shown for reference. Railway crews and train controllers identified locations by mileage as measured from Adelaide. In some cases, distances were further specified using chains (1 chain = 22 yards or 20.12 metres).

Standards and expectations have evolved significantly over time. Practices once considered acceptable and unremarkable may now be viewed as inappropriate or unsafe. Occupational health and safety, while important, did not receive the same emphasis as it does today, and environmental concerns were often secondary. Readers are encouraged to allow for these differences when engaging with the material.

During the period covered in this book, operational roles within the South Australian Railways were exclusively held by men. To preserve historical accuracy, gender-inclusive language is used sparingly and only where appropriate to the context.

Many original images featured in this book were of poor quality and have not reproduced well. Nonetheless, they have been included, as even imperfect visuals contribute to the story and help convey the atmosphere of the era.

Table of Contents

Introduction 1
1. The Peterborough Yard 3
2. The Cockburn Line 12
3. Peterborough – Ucolta 18
4. Ucolta – Oodla Wirra 27
5. Oodla Wirra – Nantabibbie 40
6. Nantabibbie – Peecharra 45
7. Peecharra – Nackara 47
8. Nackara – Methuen 58
9. Methuen – Paratoo 60
10. Paratoo – Coolawatinnie 68
11. Coolawatinnie – Yunta 72
12. Yunta – Winnininnie 79
13. Winnininnie – Oulnina 89
14. Oulnina – Mannahill 93
15. Mannahill – Wawirra 100
16. Wawirra – Outalpa 102
17. Outalpa – Olary 111
18. Olary – McDonald's Hill 121
19. McDonald's Hill – Cutana 128
20. Cutana – Mingary 133
21. Mingary – Mutooroo 147
22. Mutooroo – Cockburn 154
23. Cockburn Town 177
24. A Cockburn Stationmaster 186
25. Closing Thoughts 191
Editor's Acknowledgements 194
Bibliography 195
Index 196

*Lionel Noble in the cabin of a T-class locomotive at Mannahill, 1950 aged 25.
Photo: Lionel Noble Collection.*

*Lionel Noble March 1995.
Photo: Lionel Noble Collection.*

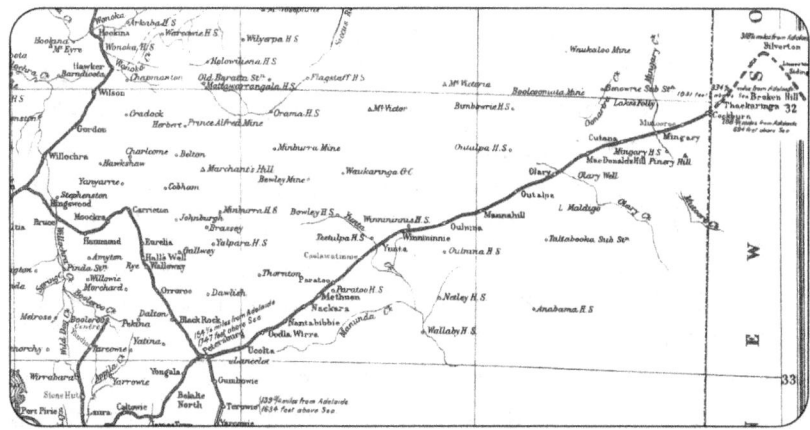

Introduction

In 1876, rich silver deposits were found in far western New South Wales, sparking an urgent need to transport the ore to a port, the nearest being Port Pirie in South Australia. A narrow-gauge line from Port Pirie to Gladstone had already opened in 1875. By January 1880 it had reached Petersburg, thereby laying the groundwork for further expansion eastwards.[1]

A July 1878 bill in the South Australian Parliament authorised a narrow-gauge extension from Terowie (the terminus of the broad-gauge line from Adelaide) to Petersburg and then onward to Quorn. From there it would link to Port Augusta and the Great Northern Line. With the existing connection to Port Pirie, Petersburg became the crossroads of multiple narrow-gauge branches by 1882: Terowie (south), Port Pirie (west), Quorn and Port Augusta (northwest), Farina on the Great Northern Line (north).

South Australia aimed to capitalise on the rapid growth of the Broken Hill and Silverton mining districts. In November

---

[1.] Petersburg's name changed to Peterborough in 1918.

The Cockburn Line

1884, the South Australian Parliament passed the Silverton Tramway Bill, authorising an extension of the railway line from Petersburg to Cockburn, situated on the New South Wales border. At Cockburn, the line connected with the privately owned Silverton Tramway Company, which facilitated the transport of ore, freight and passengers between the mining centres and broader rail networks. The narrow-gauge line reached Cockburn in 1887, and the first traffic crossed the border in early 1888.

The network radiating north, south, east and west cemented Petersburg's status as the only rail gateway to northern South Australia (and ultimately Central Australia). All these routes came under the South Australian Railways' Northern Division, with Petersburg as its operational and maintenance hub. The town boasted extensive workshops and employee housing and became one of Australia's busiest junctions—its core traffic built on Broken Hill ore.[2]

Timeline of Key Dates

- 1875 Narrow-gauge line opens from Port Pirie to Gladstone
- 1876 Silver discovered in western New South Wales
- 1880 Line reaches Petersburg
- 1882 Petersburg emerges as a junction of four narrow-gauge branches
- 1884 Silverton Tramway Bill passed, approving Petersburg – Cockburn extension
- 1887 Narrow-gauge line reaches Cockburn
- 1888 First train crosses the SA – NSW border carrying Broken Hill ore

---

[2.] The above information was gleaned from Venus, R, "Steamtown Heritage Rail Centre" (2017, Engineers Australia, Engineering Heritage SA) https://portal.engineersaustralia.org.au/system/files/engineering-heritage-australia/nomination-title/HRP.Steamtown Peterbrouugh.Nomination and report.V2.15 Nov 2017.pdf

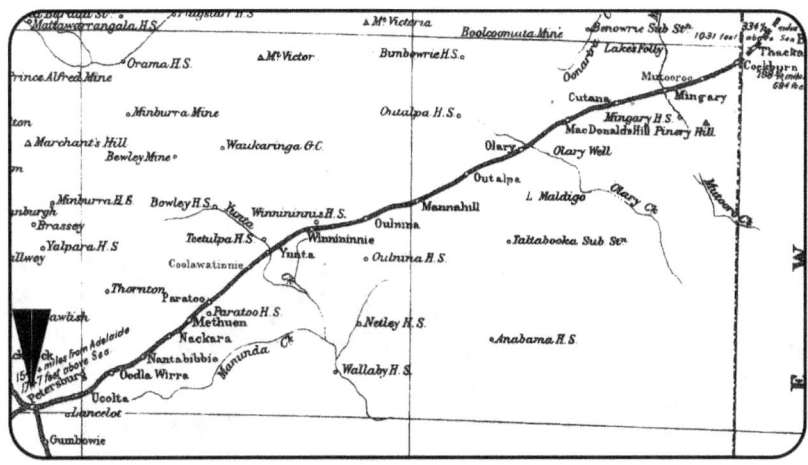

1. The Peterborough Yard

My pathway to qualify as a railway engineman began in 1942 when I was appointed as a locomotive cleaner at Adelaide's Mile End loco depot. With the war well underway, many men were taken on by the South Australian Railways (SAR) in every division. Those hoping to become firemen or enginemen started as youth locomotive cleaners and had to pass a series of examinations to progress. Everything, including out of working hours' lectures, was done for us so we could qualify to become firemen. Working all night cleaning locomotives, followed by a two-hour lecture at 9.00 am, made for a very tiring shift.

At the age of 19 in 1944, I was transferred from Mile End to Peterborough, which was a hive of industry during the war. At that time, the narrow-gauge line from Terowie to Peterborough, and then through to Quorn, was the only rail connection between Adelaide and the Northern Territory. That route was busy with troop, supply and army transport trains. The Broken Hill to Port Pirie line was equally hectic, hauling ore concentrate from the Broken Hill mines to the Port Pirie smelter. And every

The Cockburn Line

*Peterborough railway station, 1967.
Photo: Lionel Noble.*

*The yardmaster's office and bell cabin in the Peterborough
railway yard, c. 1960s. This was the operational hub of the yard.
Photo: Lionel Noble.*

1. The Peterborough Yard

line carried daily passenger traffic. It wasn't unusual for up to 100 train movements a day to pass through Peterborough. Not only was it a yardmaster's nightmare, but it was difficult for a Peterborough train crew to be given a day off; many men worked 100 or more hours per fortnight.

The bell cabin was the operating hub of the Peterborough yard. The cabin, which also housed the yardmaster's office, was an elevated room at the western end of the station precinct. From his raised position, the yardmaster could see the full extent of the yard. The large bell attached to his office was rung whenever a train left the last station before arriving at Peterborough: 4 bells signalled a train coming from Terowie, 3 from Cockburn, 2 from Port Pirie and 1 from the Quorn line. The cabin also held all the communication and signalling equipment.

Senior men told me that the first loco depot in the Peterborough yard stood at the eastern end; it was relocated to the western end after the roundhouse was built in the mid-1920s. That original eastern depot had a turntable, loco pit, overhead tank

The east end of the Peterborough traffic yard, adjacent to Railway Terrace, 1934. The original loco depot was located near the railcar turntable to the left. To the right is the SA Farmers' shed, YMCA gymnasium, YMCA hostel, the new town hall and the old town hall. The Peterborough and Railway Hotels can be seen in the distance to the top right. Photo: Lionel Noble Collection.

and water column, as well as a shed.³ The shed, which backed onto Railway Terrace, had three lines, one for passenger carriages and two for locomotives. The overhead tank was filled from a 97-foot (29.6 m) deep well adjacent to the loco pit. Water was piped from the tank to serve each line in the shed. Motor inspection cars (MIC) were housed in a shed in the same area.⁴

Peterborough loco depot looking west with Hurlstone Street crossing in the foreground, 1970. The small crossing guard's hut stands to the right. Photo: Lionel Noble.

Two railway crossings allowed movement over the yard between the northern and southern parts of the township. The eastern end crossing was on Silver Street, while Hurlstone Street marked the western end crossing. Crossing-keeper porters were employed to keep the public safe from train movements. At the east end, known as the "bell crossing", the porter operated the crossing

---

[3.] The loco pit provided engine crews access underneath the locomotive, enabling them to clean the fire and carry out essential repairs. The turntable allowed locomotives to be precisely rotated onto the appropriate track, while the water column was used to refill the locomotive tender.

[4.] Motor Inspection Cars were purposefully designed for rail operations and primarily served to transport railway officials.

1. The Peterborough Yard

The west end of the Peterborough railway yard looking east from the coal gantry, 1970. The Hurlstone Street crossing is in the centre and the small crossing porter's hut is immediately to the left of the line. Photo: Lionel Noble.

signal bells and boards by lever and set up the switches and signals for arriving and departing trains. At Hurlstone Street, electric signals weren't used. There, a porter used a kerosene lamp and a handheld stop board to protect the public during shunt and main line movements, as well as movements into and out of the locomotive depot. He was also responsible for setting up the switches for trains entering and leaving the yard. Both porters took instructions directly from the yardmaster, who decided which tracks were to be used. At night the entire yard was lit by floodlights, one on a tower adjacent to the east end crossing and another on the coal gantry at the west end. With the floodlight shining on the rails, there was never a problem spotting any vehicle during shunting.

At 4.30 pm knock-off time, the loco depot became like an ant's nest, with roughly 400 men heading home on foot, by bicycle or hopping over the fence to get into their cars. Not everyone went directly home, however, as some made a detour via the

The Cockburn Line

Peterborough loco depot looking west from the coal gantry, c. 1968. Roundhouse in the background. Photo: Lionel Noble.

hotel. I recall engineman Bill "Brumby" Jordan, known for spending time after work at the Railway Hotel on Main Street. One day, in the days when all the town's hotels closed at 6 o'clock, he came out of the hotel right at 6.00 pm, climbed onto his bicycle to ride home, and promptly fell off. He picked up his bicycle, carried it across the road, threw it over the railway fence and then loudly ordered it to, 'Stay there until you settle down a bit!' He then walked home to Peterborough West. Bill was a great man with a heart of gold.

When I first arrived at Peterborough, I was often rostered to work on the small V-class locomotive, affectionately known as "the Rat", which was used to move locomotives into and out of the roundhouse via the turntable. Two other regular shunting movements worked within the locomotive depot. The first, known as the carpenter's shunt (or "carps' shunt"), operated on the south side of the depot. This movement handled vehicles into position for repairs, servicing, oiling, air brake maintenance, painting and hot box journal replacements. The shunt

1. The Peterborough Yard

V-class locomotive 146 used for shunting in the Peterborough loco depot roundhouse, c. 1940s. Chains (foreground) were placed over the rail to prevent a movement from running into the turntable pit. WO Evans engineman. Photo: Lionel Noble Collection.

crew signed on at 5.00 am, prepared their locomotive and began shunting defective vehicles before the shed men booked on for work at 7.30 am. During the day, repaired vehicles were removed and replaced by those needing work. At the end of the day, all the repaired vehicles were marshalled into one long consist and, on the yardmaster's advice, taken into the traffic yard by the afternoon shift crew.

The second shunt was the depot shunt, which moved coal vehicles to and from the coal gantry, ash trucks from the crane removing ashes from the ash pit, coal to the boiler house and marshalling any other vehicles needed on the north side of the roundhouse. In later years, oil tankers were marshalled for use by oil-burning and diesel locomotives.

One night an unexpected incident occurred in the yard. Engineman Austin Victory and I were walking from the loco depot to the east end to begin night shunting when we heard an aeroplane, a rare sound in those days. The plane, clearly in

The Cockburn Line

trouble, had its landing lights on and was flying extremely low. We saw it try a landing on the top of the railway station, only pulling up when its lights caught a large pine tree in its path. After pulling up, it continued to fly low over Peterborough, obviously searching for a safe landing spot.

At the same time, a ball was in progress in the town hall. The police were alerted and they stopped the ball to instruct everyone with cars to at once head south to Heine Koch's paddock, arranging their headlights as a guide for the plane. The plane eventually landed safely. The next morning, I went out to the paddock and saw that it was a large Indonesian plane crewed by 5 airmen. It had been on a training flight from Victoria, and the pilot and navigator had thought they were over Port Lincoln—just a little off course! It was said that on landing they only had ten minutes' fuel left, but thankfully the air force base at Port Pirie sent fuel over and the plane took off again later that afternoon.

> **We saw it try a landing on the top of the railway station, only pulling up when its lights caught a large pine tree in its path.**

Another story from the Peterborough yard highlights the camaraderie among railway men and their love of a prank. Engineman Ray Schell once told a tale about loco storeman Mel Rowse and young employee Mervyn Olsen.

> *Mel Rowse was on all shifts at the loco depot. Poor old Merv Olsen, I remember him as if it happened yesterday. The septic pit (toilet pit) at the loco often gave trouble. It would fill up and because they didn't have motor vehicles for dispatch back then, they'd dig a pit, empty out the septic waste and pile on dirt until they had a firm top. In the meantime, they'd set up posts and a loose rope around it with two or three old kerosene lamps hanging on the posts at night.*
>
> *It was just before the railway picnic, and Mel was*

1. The Peterborough Yard

coaching Merv for the high jump event. He used to rub Merv down with black cylinder oil thinned with a bit of kerosene. 'I'm not doing any good unless there's a bit of pain in it,' Mel would say as he rubbed Merv's legs, leaving the poor fellow in pain from having his leg hair torn out.

During the last week before the picnic, Mel told Merv, 'If you can clear that rope, you'll have a pretty fair chance of winning that high jump out there at the picnic ground.'

Poor old Merv shuffled back and said, 'How much further shall I go back Mr Rowse?'

'Just a bit further,' Mel replied.

Merv got back, and when Mel said, 'That'll do.' He set off. He came in hell for leather and jumped over the rope. We didn't see him for a bit after that; he just disappeared out of sight!

Peterborough engineman and loco inspector Ray Schell, c. 1970s. Photo: Lionel Noble.

2. The Cockburn Line

For Peterborough footplate men, the Cockburn Line was the foremost line in the Peterborough Division.[5] It was the one profitable line in the SAR, thanks to its regular railing of ore concentrate from the Broken Hill mines to Port Pirie on Spencer Gulf. The privately owned Silverton Tramway Company delivered the concentrate to Burns, a railway yard next to Cockburn on the New South Wales side of the border. Locomotives were exchanged before the journey continued to the Broken Hill Proprietary (BHP) smelter at Pirie.

The Cockburn narrow-gauge line opened on 14 June 1887, with the first exchange of traffic between Cockburn and the Burns station yard taking place on 9 January 1888. The line remained open until after the last down Broken Hill express arrived at Cockburn on 10 January 1970, hauled by T-class locomotive 181.[6] The line's closure was noted in the Port Pirie *Recorder*.

> *Commencing 6.00 am on Sunday 11 January 1970, the narrow gauge and standard gauge main at Dowd's Hill (158 mile–158¾ mile) was broken and the standard gauge line re-instated by 5.00 pm. As from the time of the breaking of the track, access to the narrow-gauge line from Peterborough to Cockburn permanently ceased.[7]*

[5.] The Cockburn Line ran between Peterborough and Cockburn on the NSW border. Footplate men were the engineman and fireman.
[6.] "Down" refers to trains running from Peterborough and "up" to trains running to Peterborough.
[7.] The Recorder, Port Pirie, January 1970. Note that all distances were measured from Adelaide.

2. The Cockburn Line

Initially, the Cockburn Line was something of a mystery to me. Never having been to Cockburn, I simply saw it as a place beyond the bell crossing at the east end of the Peterborough traffic yard. When I was rostered as a fireman on the east-end shunter, part of our job was to make up the Cockburn and Terowie trains. I would often wonder about all those large timbers in the empty ore wagons arriving from Port Pirie—where were they to be used? Where were all the ore trucks and petrol tankers going? What would require such quantities? Adding to the mystery were the tired, bedraggled firemen arriving from Cockburn with blackened faces and caps rimmed by a mix of sweat and dust. Entire sides of locomotives and their tenders were covered in red dust. It was all so fascinating and it made me itch to set off into that strange wilderness.

We spent several weeks as firemen on the shunting locomotive before being rostered on the main line. A newly minted engineman was left to his own devices when working on the main line, so gaining as much practical and theoretical knowledge as possible before "graduating" was essential. The best teacher was an experienced engineman, someone like Thomas "Tim" Jenkins. Tim was a complete gentleman, always willing to help anyone who worked with him. In 1948, he compiled a notebook recording track details to help young enginemen learn their job. I remember Tim telling me the type of information he'd jotted down.

> **Adding to the mystery were the tired, bedraggled firemen arriving from Cockburn with blackened faces and caps rimmed by a mix of sweat and dust.**

The book I set up was a big help to the driver. [For example] I used to have [pertinent notes on] every section [like the one] from Peterborough to Ucolta. [Allocated running time totalled] 28 minutes: 7 minutes from

The Cockburn Line

Peterborough to the slaughterhouse crossing; 7 minutes to the next crossing which was the main road crossing this side of the tunnel; 5 minutes into the tunnel; 9 minutes from the tunnel down to Ucolta and stop in the yard. The same from Ucolta to Oodla Wirra. So much to the Lagoon crossing, so much to the 165-mile cottages, another so many minutes to the crossing in the scrub before you get to Oodla Wirra, and 19 minutes into Oodla Wirra [and so on]. So many minutes to a tree; someone chops a tree down and then they go crook at me, 'Where's the tree?'

Well-respected and highly experienced Peterborough engineman Tim Jenkins, 1975. Photo: Lionel Noble.

I always looked forward to working with Tim, not just because of what he could teach me but also because of his wit and his knack for finding humour in everyday situations. I recall him once telling me about an incident. As a running shift foreman, he had to firmly rebuke a cleaner who was shirking his duties. The cleaner got so offended he called Tim a bastard. I was shocked that anyone would say that to him. 'What did you say back?' I asked.

'I told him I would give him £10 if he could prove it,' Tim replied.

I was also fortunate to work with other senior footplate men such as Archie Williams, Fred Hill, George "Catta" Miller, Harold Mesecke and the Brennan brothers, all of whom shared valuable

2. The Cockburn Line

Peterborough engineman George "Catta" Miller, 1973. George has his locally made tucker box on his hip.

experiences and explained many interesting details about the country and the track.[8]

Tim told me a story about experienced engineman Catta Miller who was also a keen bicycle rider. In March 1914, George worked overnight to Cockburn as a fireman, signed off at 7.30 am, had breakfast and then pushed his bicycle approximately 40 miles (64 km) back to Olary. Having won the wheel race at the Olary sports that afternoon, he then rode back to Cockburn in time for his next shift to Peterborough. It's a marvel that George was still competing in cycle races at the age of 70.

Many senior enginemen regularly worked the same engine and claimed it as "theirs". Engineman Bob Dodman was very particular about his regular Yx-class locomotive 165. His attention to detail was such that he requested the cleaners not

---

[8.] George Miller's nickname came from his school days when his mates used to chant 'Miller, Miller, caterpillar.'

The Cockburn Line

only polish the superstructure but also blacken its wheels until it shone like a newly minted two-shilling ($0.20) piece. Those enginemen who claimed a regular locomotive were protective; if someone else used their engine it became a problem, especially when they went on leave. The yard was so busy that an engine couldn't be left idle for any length of time, so to prevent others from running "their" engine, they would book as many repairs as possible during their absence.

Over the years of narrow gauge operation on the Cockburn Line, there was little variation in the up and down workings. Regular down movements included passenger trains, the tucker train, the paper train, empty ore wagons, loaded fuel tankers and the produce train. Up movements included full ore trucks, empty fuel tankers and passenger trains. The produce train ran on Mondays, Wednesdays, Fridays and other days as needed, while the express passenger train ran daily both ways except on Saturdays. Goods trains were sometimes permitted to run ahead of schedule. Occasional extra movements included stock trains from Cockburn and Mannahill, as well as Broken Hill mines' Christmas holiday passenger trains.

Times for regular daily train movements were as follows:

Down Working
No. 791 Passenger to Cockburn. Depart 12.18 am.
No. 251 Tucker train. Depart 8.00 am. Performed shunts en route.
No. 419 Paper train. Depart 3.10 pm.
No. 503 Usually empty ore and loaded fuel tankers for Broken Hill.
No. 531 Produce train. This train took beer and perishables from Mile End, departing there around midday. Depart Peterborough around 9.30 pm.

The load for down freight trains was 378 tons.

2. The Cockburn Line

Up Working
No. 228 Freight. Usually a full load of ore. Depart 6.55 am.
No. 270 Freight. Performed shunt movements en route as required. Depart 840 am.
No. 306 Freight. Empty fuel tanks and ore. Depart 10.25 am.
No. 360 Freight. Full load of ore. Depart 12.30 pm.
No. 440 Freight. Full load of ore. Depart 3.50 pm.
No. 222 Passenger. Depart 9.34 pm.
No. 612 Freight. Full load of ore. Depart 11.00 pm.

The load for freight trains ex-Cockburn was 526 tons to Paratoo, reduced to 410 tons from there to Peterborough.

The Peterborough timetable book No. 124 of 1923 provides a good indication of how busy the line was back then. For instance, one up train from Cockburn was scheduled to cross at least 10 other trains en route. In 1923, the open stations where such crossings occurred were Ucolta, Oodla Wirra, Nantabibbie, Nackara, Methuen, Paratoo, Yunta, Winnininnie, Oulnina, Mannahill, Outalpa, Olary, McDonald's Hill, Cutana, Mingary, Mutooroo and Cockburn. Train speeds through station yards were 15 mph (24 kph), and speed entering the Peterborough yard dropped to 8 mph (13 kph). Railway refreshment rooms were located at Peterborough, Mannahill and Cockburn. Triangles for turning locomotives were at Paratoo and Mingary, and turntables were at Peterborough, Mannahill and Cockburn. Watering columns were stationed at all the main stops.

It wasn't long after I arrived in Peterborough when, at age 20, I finally got my first trip to Cockburn. I was rostered on the paper train, which carried newspapers and consumables to stations along the line. Railway employees and residents from the small communities along the track would write or call Peterborough businesses to place orders, which were then loaded onto the train for those further up. I couldn't wait!

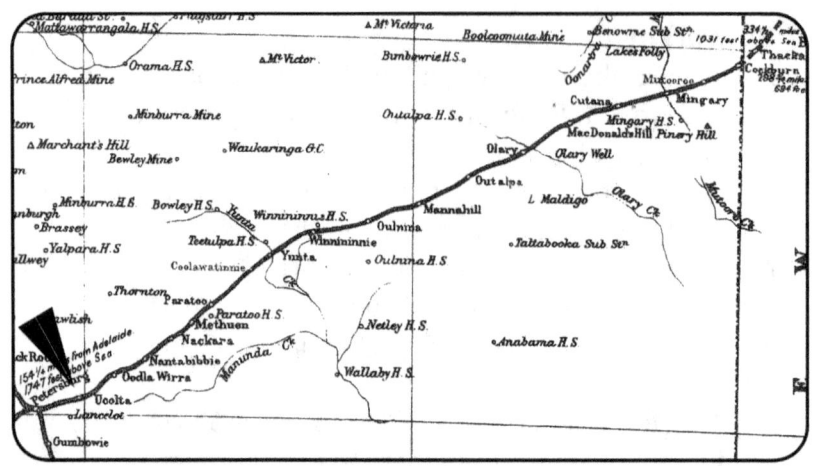

3. Peterborough – Ucolta

Ucolta was 8 miles (12.9 km) from Peterborough

The name Ucolta was recorded in the 1860s by government surveyor Joseph Brooks. Early district resident James Thyer believed it derived from the indigenous name "Eucolta" for nearby Flagstaff Hill. Although Peterborough and Ucolta sit at much the same height above sea level, with Peterborough at 1 747 feet (532.5 m) and Ucolta at 1 745 feet (532.9 m), between the two stands Dowd's Hill (1 916 feet or 584 m) with its railway tunnel. The grade up Dowd's Hill meant steam locomotives had to get a few extra shovels of coal into the firebox to make the climb before steaming on to Ucolta.

The first point of interest on the main line to Ucolta was Yankee Dip on the outskirts of Peterborough. Yankee Dip was a low-lying area where a water course ran under the line, allowing floodwaters from the Gumbowie and Sunnybrae areas to bypass the town. I remember, as a fireman, only once passing through Yankee Dip when water was flowing, and it was a small amount then. Old enginemen told me that when the water was high

3. Peterborough – Ucolta

*Ucolta railway station, c. 1920s. Note the milk/cream cans.
Photo: Mrs Jago (Terowie).*

enough to cover the tender axle boxes, they had to stop immediately after passing through and empty the water from the boxes with a special syringe. Many trains were delayed at Peterborough waiting for the water to subside, and later diesel-electric locomotives were not permitted to pass through when water was above the rails.

An incident occurred at Yankee Dip shortly after the new Australians had arrived on the Division.[9] I was a fireman qualified to drive and was rostered as engineman on a down Cockburn trip with a young, eager Estonian chap. We had just passed through Yankee Dip when a gauge glass suddenly burst, filling the cabin with steam.[10] In such an emergency, either the engineman or the fireman needed to close the gauge glass cocks by

---

[9.] In December 1951, 447 migrants, mostly of German origin, arrived to be trained as train crew and signalmen for the SAR. Among them were 337 young single men. The recruitment effort was led by CH Fidock, the Welfare Officer and Railways Institute Secretary, who also identified potential migrants in Great Britain, Holland, Italy and Malta.

[10.] Typically installed above the firebox door, the gauge glass allowed the crew to check the boiler's water level quickly and safely. Constructed from specially tempered, thick glass in a square design, it was engineered to withstand the extreme pressures within the boiler.

The Cockburn Line

pulling a chain on their side. I closed the cocks on my side but, as steam continued to fill the cab, I reached over and closed the chain on the fireman's side too. When the steam finally cleared, I found myself alone in the cabin! I looked toward the front and rear along my mate's side, and there he was on the bank watching the brake van go past. It was his first broken gauge glass experience, and the shock was so great that he jumped off, leaving me to manage by myself.

Senior engineman Tim Jenkins later told me about his own Yankee Dip experience:

> *My mate Harry Foster and I came home from Cockburn on a 600 up this morning and we were coming down to Yankee Dip at about 10.00 am. We could see water over the track, but nothing had been said about it. Train control usually let us know at Ucolta if the Yankee Dip was full and warned us to take precautions. The down grade from the slaughterhouse to Yankee Dip was pretty heavy and we were sliding down with no chance of stopping. There was only one thing to do. 'Shut the damper, Harry,' I said. I shut the gauge cocks, and we went through the water at 20 mph (32 kph). The cowcatcher split the water straight over the top of us, some of which lobbed back into the next truck. I was very concerned that no one in Peterborough had told us about it. The old Yankee Dip used to cause a lot of bother when you got a flash flood from Gumbowie.*

Dowd's Hill tunnel opened in early 1898, and between there and Peterborough were four level crossings, mostly for farm access. Near the third crossing on an up movement, the engineman would blow the challenging whistle to alert the traffic employees (and their wives) that a train from Cockburn was on the

3. Peterborough – Ucolta

T-class locomotive 248 exiting Dowd's Hill tunnel on the Peterborough side, c. 1920s. Note no headlight and the old type pilot and tender.
Photo: L Rasmus.

Ucolta railway reservoir and pump house, c. 1920s. Note the old Dawson Road cottages to the left which were there prior to the construction of the narrow-gauge yard.
Photo: Mrs Jago (Terowie).

outskirts. The crossing keeper would then clear the signals. Near the fourth level crossing, the body of a man murdered many years ago in Peterborough was said to have been buried by his murderer.

A little peep on the whistle, either just before or just after passing the tunnel at Dowd's Hill, would prompt a wave from Mrs Malycha or Mrs Cummings, the farmer's wives on respective farms each side of the tunnel. Once we had passed through the tunnel on a down movement, the fireman could finally take a short rest as the grade to Ucolta was gentle. Two more level crossings were after Dowd's Hill before finally reaching Ucolta.

There was a large overhead tank and a water column near the centre of the yard at Ucolta, although Oodla Wirra served as the

Ucolta railway picnic train. Roy Hogg guard, Jack McKay engineman, Harry Petropolous fireman. Photo: Lionel Noble.

3. Peterborough – Ucolta

main watering station. Water was taken at Ucolta only when there was a shortage at Oodla Wirra. Water to both the overhead tank and the neighbouring employee cottages was pumped by a steam-operated pump from two nearby reservoirs.

Ucolta's Amelia Park recreation ground was the venue for the annual Peterborough railway picnic. Picnic trains started from Peterborough West, passed through the main station, and continued to Amelia Park, located next to the last level crossing before the Ucolta yard. The October picnic was a yearly highlight for the children, with many railway employees and their families along the Cockburn Line also attending. For families further up the line, a passenger car was attached to a freight train that left Cockburn around 11.00 pm the night before, arriving at Amelia Park the following morning. They returned in a carriage attached to the paper train, which departed Peterborough at 3.00 pm. It was a long day for everyone.

I remember Ucolta resident Les Rasmus telling me about the hundreds of wheat bags stacked at the siding when he was a young

The popular ocean wave at Peterborough railway picnic at Amelia Park, c. 1964. Photo: Lionel Noble.

The Cockburn Line

Ucolta railway yard, c. 1950s. Loaded wheat bags to the left and water column at the centre. Employee cottage to the right. Photo: Lionel Noble Collection.

man. Each bag was weighed on a simple set of scales and handled manually. In season, a loaded wheat train would depart each day.

Signalmen Tom Walsh and Bob Cornwell were stationed at Ucolta. Both were very keen on their jobs, but one was a little too clever for his own good. He discovered how to draw two or more electric staffs from a single machine, and one day he demonstrated this ability to a railway officer.[11] He was promptly dismissed!

Many years ago, I was firing for engineman Archie Williams on an up freight train on the rising grade to the tunnel when we encountered grasshoppers on the line. At that stage the insects were small and just hopping, but that's when they caused the most trouble for a train. Millions of them were on the line, and by the time we neared the tunnel, the locomotive wheels had

---

[11.] The electric staff signalling system was designed to ensure that only one train could occupy a specific block section at any given time. For safety reasons it wasn't permitted, nor supposedly possible, to remove more than one staff at a time. The metal staff itself, typically strapped to a bamboo hoop, had to be carried on the locomotive as its permission to be on that section of the track.

3. Peterborough – Ucolta

been slipping for quite a while. I was jumping in and out of the cab, shovelling dirt under the driving wheels to try and gain enough grip to make the grade. We even tied a bag onto the cowcatcher to sweep the rail, but nothing worked. It took so long to clear the grade that we eventually had to return to Ucolta to fill the tender with water. We spent five hours on just that section and it added up to a nineteen-hour-plus shift in all.

Beginning construction of the new Dowd's Hill tunnel for standardisation, 1971. The tunnel facilitated an overpass for the realigned main road.
Photo: Lionel Noble.

The Cockburn Line

*The new Oodla Wirra railway station, c. 1920s.
L: G Moller, Fred Woolcock (Stationmaster),
Cecil and Charlie Woods. Photo: L Rasmus.*

*Drew's Well, Ucolta. The pipe was used to temporarily pump water
to the overhead tank in the Ucolta railway yard. Photo: L Rasmus*

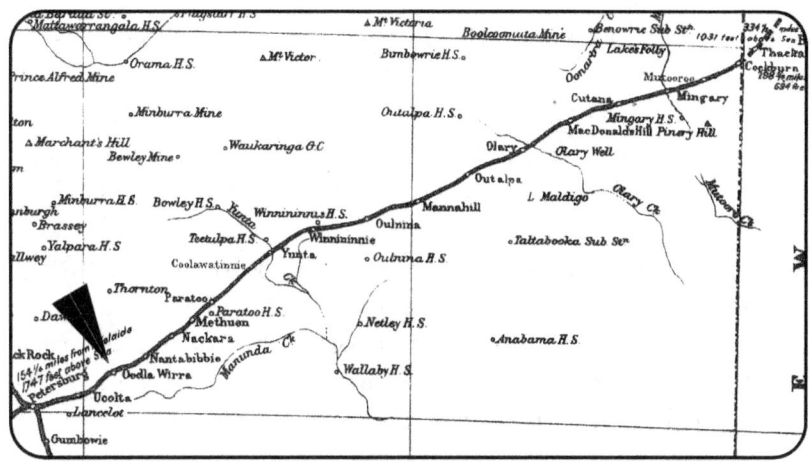

4. Ucolta – Oodla Wirra

Oodla Wirra was 7½ miles (12.1 km) from Ucolta and 15½ miles (25 km) from Peterborough

According to *Manning's Place Names of South Australia* (2006), the name Oodla Wirra is said to derive from one of two possible indigenous words: "ngurlewirra" meaning "hill frost" or "judlawirra" meaning "kangaroo forest". Surveyor Brooks noted that "oodla" (or "odloo") referred to kangaroo, while "wirra" meant gum tree, giving it the literal sense of "gumtree country inhabited by kangaroo". The station stood at 1 657 feet (505.1 m) above sea level.

After leaving Ucolta, four level crossings were along the section. The first was the Broken Hill road crossing, which the train crews called the main road crossing. Next came Dann's crossing, named after Alf Dann, who had a farm on the right-hand side near the crossing. The third was the school crossing, where local children were picked up and dropped off. The final crossing was known as the cemetery crossing and lay very near the Oodla Wirra distant signal. The small, secluded

The Cockburn Line

cemetery on the right-hand side of the line contained roughly 40 graves.

A farmhouse and its adjacent tennis courts stood on the right when leaving the Ucolta yard. As a child I lived in Peterborough, and back then the farm belonged to a Mr Jacobs who was a friend of my parents. When visiting the Jacobs, I could hear the trains making their way up the grade from Oodla Wirra, then shutting off steam for the slight downhill run into Ucolta station. A pumping shed next to the tennis courts drew water from the 140-foot-deep Drew's Well and, during a water shortage in the early thirties, water from the well was piped to the railway's overhead tank.

600-class double header on the line through Hutton's Lagoon Ucolta, 1973. Mark Noble in foreground.
Photo: Lionel Noble.

The standard-gauge track through the filled Hutton's Lagoon Ucolta, 1973.
Photo: Lionel Noble.

4. Ucolta – Oodla Wirra

Not far from Ucolta, a section of the track ran alongside Hutton's Lagoon, a spot named after a progressive local farmer whose 300-acre (121.4 ha) property was mostly underwater when the lagoon was full. The lagoon became a popular venue for regattas, boating, picnicking and swimming. Hutton even dug 500-foot-long channels to carry windmill-pumped water from the lagoon so he could grow his successful lucerne crop. When the lagoon dried, the bed also produced a fine wheat crop.

The overhead water tank on the Cockburn line near Hutton's Lagoon at Ucolta, c. 1920. Photo: L Rasmus.

As early as 1890, the lagoon was known to fill and spread to both sides of the line. When full, its average depth reached 3 feet 6 inches (1.1 m) and it boasted a capacity of 186 214 552 gallons (704 898 759 L). Around 1891, an overhead tank and pump house were installed adjacent to the narrow-gauge line on the north side of the lagoon. A government-built whip well, constructed long before the rail line, also stood in the vicinity on the early stock route between Terowie, Lancelot (just south of Ucolta) and Traveller's Rest (just north of Oodla Wirra).

There were rarely any problems firing or driving a train between Ucolta and Oodla Wirra. After climbing the gentle grade past the lagoon, perhaps one or two extra firings were all that was needed to reach Oodla Wirra, where water was nearly always added to the tender.

Arriving at Oodla Wirra required careful judgement when entering from the Ucolta end; the longer the train's consist the more care was needed. As the engineman entered the railway yard, he would close the regulator some distance from the distant signal and prepare to handle the train down the slight grade. On T-class locomotives operating before air braking, the fireman would slightly screw on the tender hand brake to gradually bunch the vehicles as each began its descent. That action alleviated slack and allowed for a smooth stop.

> **In the air brake era, the most important point for an engineman to remember was that the safest stop came when the brake pipe was fully charged with air.**

In the air brake era, the most important point for an engineman to remember was that the safest stop came when the brake pipe was fully charged with air. When entering the Oodla Wirra yard, the train was always slowed through a brake pipe air reduction achieved by releasing a small amount of air from the locomotive's equalising reservoir. For a freight train, it was essential to have the train pipe fully charged before making the final stop in the yard.

The original wooden station building at Oodla Wirra was burnt to the ground around 1925 when porter Barney Sheehan left the lights burning as he went off duty for his evening meal. Peterborough resident Harcourt Rawlins recalled that the water in the large, galvanised tank adjacent to the burning building boiled from the fire's intense heat. For quite some time

4. Ucolta – Oodla Wirra

Oodla Wirra railway station staff, c. 1930s.
L to R: Chris Howard, Jack Medlin, Tom McCabe.
Photo: Lionel Noble Collection.

Bullock teams hauling firewood being loaded onto vehicles at Oodla Wirra, c. 1900s. The original wooden railway station is to the right. Photo: M. Rawlins.

afterwards, all railway business was conducted in the waiting shed until the new stone station building opened. Oodla Wirra station finally closed on 1 November 1968.

Oodla Wirra served as a crew relief point. On the up trip from Cockburn, it wasn't uncommon for train crews to be on duty for long hours. When that happened, a crew would be sent on a down train from Peterborough to take over, with the relieved crew then riding in the brake van back to Peterborough. It was also an important siding for carting firewood, with horse and bullock teams bringing in the wood from outlying areas to be loaded. I remember Ben Hucks, a Nantabibbie farmer born in 1889 and who later settled at Oodla Wirra, telling me about the time he saw 144 bullocks in the yard, yoked up and ready to load wood. The ruins of the old two-storey flour mill, where 6 men were employed, stood just outside the railway fence at the Parnaroo Road corner.

Flooding was always a challenge at Oodla Wirra. Tom Fitzgerald wrote about a conversation he'd had with resident Pat Daley, who recalled New Year's Day in 1889 when heavy rains caused considerable damage to railway property. Pat told Tom

Flooding at Oodla Wirra, 1941. Photo: L Rasmus.

4. Ucolta – Oodla Wirra

that they'd gone 12 months without any rain until that fateful day when 9 inches (228.6 mm) fell, filling Hutton's Lagoon for the first time in 20 years. All traffic on the Cockburn Line was suspended for over a week, and rising floodwaters in town surrounded the railway cottages, so much so that a child was tragically found drowned in a bedroom.

Pat, who was then a signalman at Oodla Wirra, discovered that the railway bridge between his home and the distant signal had been swept away. Wading through the water, he waved a red light to stop an up train from danger. A flash of lightning then lit up the line, disclosing the peril ahead to the locomotive crew. After a story about the event appeared in the local press, the engineman found himself on the carpet. He was charged with having communicated with the press, contrary to railway rules. He denied the charge, but resigned from the service anyhow, feeling he was a marked man.

Nantabibbie farmers Ben and Edie Hucks at Oodla Wirra, 1973. Photo: Lionel Noble.

The Cockburn Line

According to Ben Hucks, 10 inches (254 mm) of rain fell in the area in 1929. The resulting floods swept the gangers' trolley shed away, with sleepers from the shed ending up on Alf Dann's property 8 miles (13 km) to the south. The porter's house was flooded, his piano was seen floating around his house and all the house contents were spoilt. Ben also said:

> *I was starved out then and went into the railway in 1929. I lost horses, cows. They put every person they could in the railway then. No gravel (line ballast) left; swept away. From the mill to the hall was under water. The flood swept everything away. That is how the 'yunta curse' (weed with a yellow flower) came down here first. They carted the ballast down and the weed came with the ballast from Yunta. All the water runs through to Meadow Downs Station. I worked in the railway for a month or six weeks and was paid £100 to feed 4 cows which I used for milk and butter when May (daughter) was born. Hard times.*

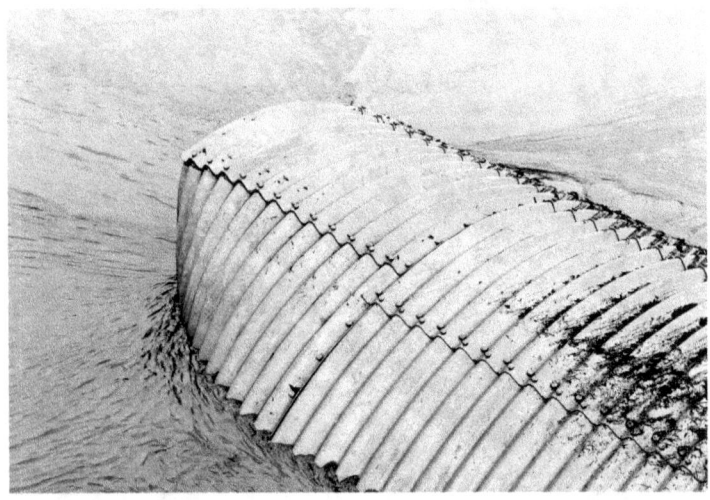

A large flood-damaged pipe on the standard-gauge line at Hill Grange near Oodla Wirra, 1973. Photo: Lionel Noble.

4. Ucolta – Oodla Wirra

On 9 September 1889 a flux mine was opened by John Heithersay of Petersburg near Mt Grainger, connected to the main line at Oodla Wirra by a horse-drawn tramway. X-class vehicles ran on their own down the grade to the mine, and two draught horses hauled roughly four truckloads each day back to the station, from where the ore was sent on to Port Pirie. The mine provided work for 30 to 40 men but eventually ceased operations when the Iron Knob mine opened.

NSW railway historian Alex Grunbach investigating the old track formation for the tramway to the Oodla Wirra flux mine, 1974. Photo: Lionel Noble

Standing next to the loco pit on the eastern side of the railway yard was the emergency sand tank, used for filling the sand boxes on the locomotives. The sand boxes were often filled at Oodla Wirra, especially whenever the locomotive wheels had been slipping on the grade from Nackara to Nantabibbie. Slipping could be caused by all sorts of things: grasshoppers, grease or oil dropped on the rail head, a rail that turned wet then dry after a shower, little white snails that settled on the rail overnight or even an incorrectly adjusted rail greaser machine. The engineman tried to eliminate the slip by operating the sand lever in conjunction with the regulator and the reversing gear.

After a 46-minute climb from Nackara to Nantabibbie on an up movement, and particularly if the coal wasn't up to standard, it became necessary to clean the fire in the Oodla Wirra loco depot ash pit. Large clinkers often formed on the back grates of the firebox and had to be pushed forward over the grates and out through the dead-plate opening at the front.[12] If no pit was available, the ashes from the front pan had to be cleared through the spokes of the locomotive wheel, meaning you'd have to lie on your stomach between the engine and the tender to reach the rear end of the pan. We had no electric lights to help with the job, mind you.

One time I was firing for Ralph Watson. We'd been working all night from Cockburn and, as soon as we arrived at Oodla Wirra, Ralph noticed fire in the ash pan before we'd cleaned it. We cleaned the pan and then found, on closer examination, that the grate-operating rod pin under the grates had fallen out and was nowhere to be found. We cooled the pan down using the ash pan wetter, then I did what I'd seen the boilermakers do at the Peterborough loco depot—put my head and arms right into the pan to make some temporary repairs by jamming a worn dog spike in position to hold the grates secure. Not a very nice job to be sure, especially with the fire still on the back grates and dead plate.

Very often, water tanks were filled at Oodla Wirra for the ganger's supply along the Cockburn Line. Drinking water was normally tanked from Gladstone, while travelling tanks were filled from the overhead tank in the Oodla Wirra yard. This overhead tank was supplied by two reservoirs with a combined

---

[12.] Clinker was a glass-like molten mass formed by impurities in coal. It stuck to the firebox grates and inhibited airflow to the fire.

4. Ucolta – Oodla Wirra

Filling 3000 gallon water tanks at Oodla Wirra. Guard Bruce McPherson on the water tank and Peterborough fireman Guenter Teske in the foreground, c. 1950s. Guenter was from Germany, having come out to Australia to work after WW II. Photo: Lionel Noble.

Taking on water at the Oodla Wirra narrow-gauge railway yard looking south, c. 1950s. Photo: Lionel Noble.

capacity of over 12 million gallons (45 424 941 L). The rainfall and runoff were such that there was always plenty to go around; I don't ever recall having to cart water to Oodla Wirra. Engineman Gordon Miller used to tell me about one of the reservoirs under construction around 1901–03, when workers discovered the remains of a *Diplodocus* dinosaur about 30 feet (9 m) below the present ground level. The bones were sent to the Adelaide Museum.

I was working as engineman on a T-class locomotive attached to a 400-class Garrett, and we were taking water on the passing siding at Oodla Wirra. My fireman had filled our tender, and because the 400-class was running with the large water tank leading, he left the water column chute over the T-class tender filler inlet. Meanwhile, the fireman on the 400-class had already got himself ready to start off. When I sounded the whistle to move ahead, for some reason the engineman on the 400-class took it for a "right away" signal and smartly opened the regulator on his locomotive, shooting off. The 400-class fireman grabbed the column chute but was pushed aside and ended up swinging on it parallel to the track. When the movement finally stopped, he was helped off the chute onto the 400-class cabin roof, which by then was directly opposite.

Another incident occurred on 5 August 1953 at that same water column. I was on my first trip as an engineman, under the instruction of loco inspector Herb Nelson on a 400-class locomotive with fireman Kurt Postler. We'd learned the Westinghouse air brake and had passed our examinations back in 1948, though at that time no locomotives in Peterborough were fitted with that type of brake equipment. As we approached Oodla Wirra, I planned to stop near the water column on my mate's side of the locomotive. You had to guess

4. Ucolta – Oodla Wirra

when your mate would call 'Stop!' as the column passed the cabin, and the fireman also had to time the stop so that the water column lined up perfectly with the inlet.

As we entered the yard, Herb suggested he get into the driver's seat to show me how to make a good stop. There he was, looking all stern and serious—that inspector's look—when suddenly my fireman yelled, 'Stop!' His yell startled Herb so badly he nearly jumped out of his seat. Once the train halted, my fireman cheekily asked, 'Where do you want it, Mr Nelson? In the first or second truck?' He'd gone right past the column! I had to climb out of the cabin because I was laughing so hard at Kurt's cheeky comment.

Oodla Wirra permanent way railway employees, 1967.
L to R: K Evans, N Jackson and J Duchoslav (packers),
and Graham Thomas (ganger). Photo: Lionel Noble.

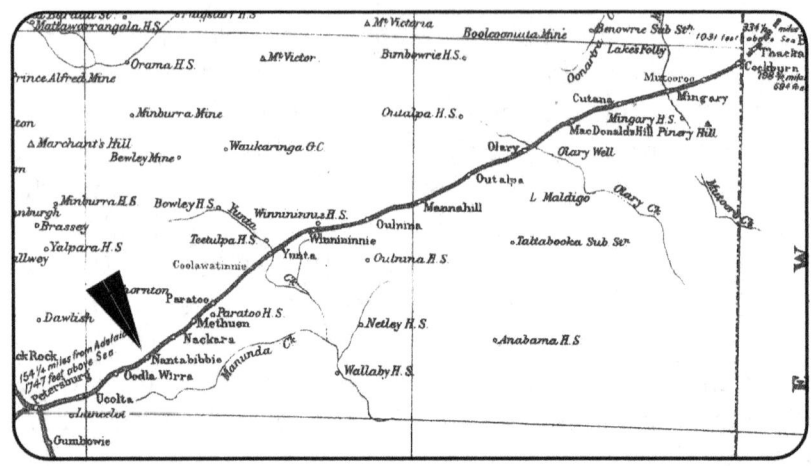

5. Oodla Wirra – Nantabibbie

Nantabibbie was 5¾ miles (9.25 km) from Oodla Wirra and 21¼ miles (34 km) from Peterborough

The name of the Nantabibbie siding came from the indigenous word for a black kangaroo; the station opened in 1898 and closed on 1 August 1963. The original station faced the Broken Hill main road with a full-length veranda on the road side; the building was removed in 1930. In my time, the only structure in sight was a small station humpy, just big enough to house two telephones, the train order and register books and two electric staff instruments. A porter named Jack Kosh was the first porter/stationmaster at Nantabibbie, and he lived there for many years. That section of track demanded extra effort from the fireman, climbing from 1 657 feet (505 m) above sea level at Oodla Wirra to 1 808 feet (551 m) at Nantabibbie. No water columns or locomotive pits were in the yard.

There were three level crossings along that stretch. The first was immediately after leaving Oodla Wirra and gave access to

5. Oodla Wirra – Nantabibbie

Nantabibbie railway station, c. 1910s. The veranda faced the main Broken Hill road and the station was removed in 1930. Photo: Lionel Noble Collection.

the Hillgrange and Parnaroo areas. The second was on the grade, not far from the 174-mile cutting. From the top of that cutting, the line dipped down before pulling up slightly into the Nantabibbie yard, passing over the third level crossing before reaching the yard proper. That last crossing was on the old main road to Nackara, used long before the current Broken Hill road came into being.

The curved passing siding and main lines in the Nantabibbie yard made signalling a challenge, so a 44-gallon drum painted white was used to mark when the rear of the train was clear of the trailing points. Shunting at Nantabibbie was a tricky business, and vehicles on up-working trains were mostly detached and re-attached. There was also a small spur freight line (removed in 1959) with a dead end where firewood, sheep and wool were loaded.

The original line formation ran along the east side of the main Broken Hill road up to a point behind the old station

The Cockburn Line

Camp for the workers who worked on the change of grade project between Nackara, Peecharra and Nantabibbie, 1903. The camp was near the Nantabibbie farm of Ben Hucks. Photo: Lionel Noble Collection.

Members of the railway work gang who worked on the change of grade between the S-bend between Peecharra and Nantabibbie, 1903. Jim Kendell (far right) and Jack Teague (squatting third from right). The young boys provided water for the workers so they could continue working. Photo: Ben Hucks.

5. Oodla Wirra – Nantabibbie

building. It branched off from the original narrow-gauge line at what the footplate men called the "S bend" and headed northwest through Mercer's paddock, eventually running alongside the main road. You can still see the remains of a culvert from that original line on the east side of the road. Looking across from the new formation over to the old embankment, the grade appears very steep; I can easily imagine the difficulty of climbing it in bad weather.

The section was undulating, with plenty of dips along the way to the top cutting at the 174-mile mark. That cutting was deepened around 1901–1903 because the grade was too severe for Y-class locomotives which would slip due to grasshoppers and adverse weather conditions. Nantabibbie farmer Ben Hucks remembered when they deepened the cutting. Seventy to eighty men were on it, and they even regraded the track from Nackara to Nantabibbie. At that time, a three-year drought was in full swing, and many local men were drafted into the construction gang under foreman Jim Kendell. The workers' camp had a shop run by a Mr Abottomey which, as Ben put it, 'kept every mortal thing' for the men. They cooked, ate and slept in their own tents with very few facilities, 'a bush toilet with a big hole dug out'.

Just over a high bridge outside the yard limit board at the Peecharra end of the yard, a huge rock balanced on a shelf close to the line. They used dynamite in regrading the cutting, and one of the explosions had blasted the rock up to that spot, where it stayed until the narrow-gauge line closed. Mick Casey, a long-time member of the Ucolta permanent way gang, even chiselled his name on it. The humpy where they stored the explosives remained on the Oodla Wirra side of the cutting, right by the Hucks' farm fence.

I was working that section as a young fireman with engineman Harold Mesecke. We were doing all the odd jobs,

The Cockburn Line

from unloading drinking water and ballast to shunting and dropping off chaff for horse teams working along the track or at the reservoirs. Harold, a genuine bushman, hopped off the locomotive halfway up to Nantabibbie and pulled some branches off a wattle tree. He then brought the branches back to the cabin and stuffed them in a bag. As a young fireman, I didn't question it. Later, back home in Peterborough, one of the other chaps asked how I'd gotten on with Harold, to which I said I had no complaints. He then asked if Harold had collected any wattle branches on the way up to Nanty. That gave me a chance to ask why. It turns out Harold used wattle bark for tanning kangaroo skin. He made and sold kangaroo purses using the two lower objects of a buck kangaroo—cut off, cleaned out and tanned. He added a silver snap clip, and the purse sold for 5 shillings ($0.50). Harold also had another quirky habit. For some reason, while the train was slowly chugging uphill, he would get off and walk onto the footplate with a huge spanner tightening up nuts.

On Ben Huck's farm at Nantabibbie, May 1973. The humpy was used by railway construction workers in 1903 to store explosives when the 174-mile railway cutting was being deepened. Photo: Lionel Noble.

Entering the Nantabibbie railway yard from the Peecharra end, c. 1960s. The large rock to the left was lodged there during construction of the cutting when 10 charges of dynamite were used. Photo: Lionel Noble.

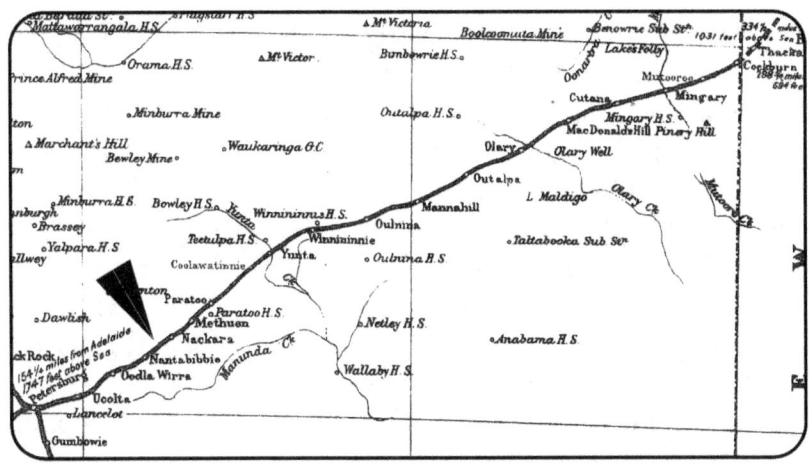

6. Nantabibbie – Peecharra

Peecharra was 2½ miles (4 km) from Nantabibbie and 23¾ miles (38 km) from Peterborough

Peecharra railway station opened on 12 September 1928 with a passing siding and a small shed, and it closed in 1959. I often wondered why they built Peecharra when it was only 2 miles (3.2 km) from Nantabibbie and 4½ miles (7.25 km) from Nackara. Nantabibbie sat 1 808 feet (551 m) above sea level, while Peecharra was slightly lower at 1 801 feet (549 m). A down freight train would cover the distance in 7 minutes, but an up movement took 19 minutes.

It was a 1-in-80 down grade from Nantabibbie to Peecharra, so the fireman had little to do except bunch the train using the tender hand brake, and even then, only when the engineman advised it. The Peecharra yard was on a grade not much different from that at Nantabibbie. The ground on either side of the passing siding was clear, making it a popular spot during footy season for the footballers to jump off and have a run alongside the locomotive cabin.

The Cockburn Line

A railway reservoir that supplied the Nackara overhead tank was built to the right of the siding. It was the only reservoir in the area and was 27 feet 3 inches (8.3 m) deep, holding 16 101 900 gallons (60 952 322 L) when full. According to Ben Hucks, they had continual problems with it because, being dug into sand, it didn't retain water. I remember many chaff bags being offloaded to feed the horse teams hired for removing silt. To try and fix the issue, they lined the dam in 1950 with clay from Eurelia and even used 3 000 sheep to trample it. It wasn't successful. Later, a bulldozer was used to reshape the reservoir, but that spoiled it completely and, from then on, it emptied about as quickly as it filled.

Signalman's house and station buildings in the Nackara railway yard, 1948.
Photo: Lionel Noble Collection.

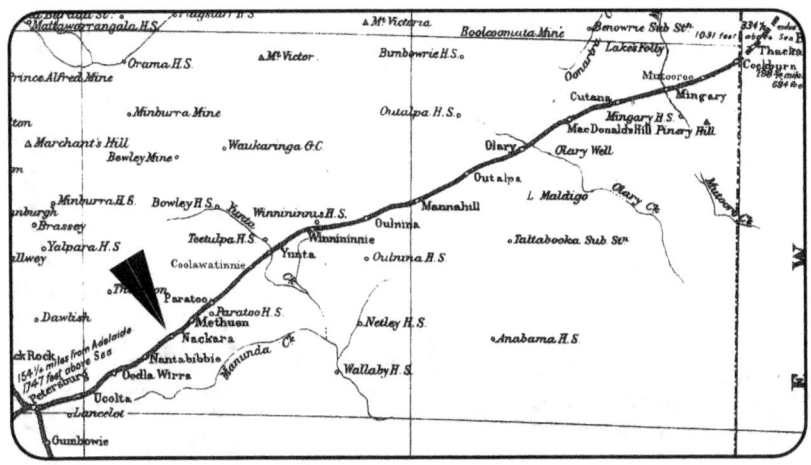

7. Peecharra – Nackara

Nackara was 4½ miles (7.25 km) from Peecharra and 28¼ miles (48.5 km) from Peterborough

According to Manning, the name Nackara may have come from the indigenous word "nakkare", the name of a game forbidden during initiation ceremonies. With a fall of 380 feet (115.8 m) in height above sea level between Peecharra at 1 801 feet (549 m) and Nackara at 1 421 feet (433.2 m), all that was needed to get a train moving from Peecharra was to release the brakes, and it would run itself to Nackara. The scheduled running time for a down freight train from Peecharra to Nackara was 11 minutes, whereas an up train took 29 minutes because it was uphill all the way. Many a fireman on up movements wished that the yard limit board would bob up sooner, especially when battling a locomotive that wasn't steaming well or wasn't fed good-quality coal. For up trains there was a slight break in the grade at the S-bend, which allowed the train to stop for a bit to build up steam and top up the boiler water if necessary.

The Cockburn Line

Y-class locomotive travelling towards Peecharra on the S-bend between Nackara and Peecharra. Photo: Lionel Noble.

Three level crossings were on this section. The first was over the main Broken Hill road and was one where accidents often occurred. I still recall one night when a car smashed into the side of a moving up train. The second crossing was on the S-curve down near Mercer's paddock, on that part of the line where the present formation deviated from the old one. That crossing was busy too, mostly used by local farmers. The third crossing was at the top of a long, straight stretch of track running right into the Nackara yard.

Where a station was attended, the signalman in charge would ride his cycle to the yard switches, set the road and clear the signals. If the station didn't have fixed signals, then the signalman or porter at the facing switches would have to wave a large hand-signal flag to the engineman entering the yard. The instruction came from the train controller and was acknowledged by a short "peep" on the whistle. If two trains arrived at the same time, the controller decided which was given preference.

7. Peecharra – Nackara

From as far back as 1886, the small Nackara siding was a very busy place. There must have been many rail travellers in the early days as the rail-level passenger platform was even widened in 1900. I remember the 1950s as years when there was plenty of activity around Nackara and on the railway. All the railway cottages were occupied and many children attended the school. Cars would often pass over the road crossing at the Methuen end of the yard while heading to or from the post office/store; on Saturdays stock was loaded or unloaded on railway trucks and the tennis courts were full of players.

Staff shed at Nackara railway yard, 1964.
(L to R): Rodney Smith, ganger ? White, Robert Adams.
Photo: Lionel Noble.

Wheat was grown in the Nackara area until about 1918, when vermin and kangaroos moved in. In the very early days of settlement, up to four wheat agents' huts stood along the west side of the yard, the last of which—Darling and Co.—was removed in 1893. Ben Hucks said that the early years brought excellent crops. Primary production wasn't limited to wheat; I also heard about a farmer by the name of Tietz who sowed turnips between rows of wheat. Most local farmers also milked cows, and a large brake van would come daily from Paratoo to pick up milk and cream along the route to Peterborough.

400-class locomotive 409 taking on water at Nackara while crossing 830-class 840. Lionel Noble in the cabin of 409.
Photo: Lionel Noble Collection.

On arriving at Nackara on an up movement, ten minutes were allocated for locomotive pit work. Firemen didn't usually carry a watch at that time, many didn't own one, but they kept an eye on the engineman's. His was a large pocket watch, usually hung on a hook on his side of the cabin and cushioned with a wad of wool waste to protect it from vibration. After cleaning the fire and taking on water, it was important to get off to a good start, with a well-burning fire, a full head of steam and, above all, a boiler run so clean that priming didn't occur.[13] The old senior enginemen used to say, 'A good start, a good finish.'

[13.] Priming occurred when boiler water entered the steam delivery system and was expelled through the funnel. This could cause significant damage to the locomotive.

7. Peecharra – Nackara

Because of the grade, down running on this section gave the fireman little to do besides maybe washing his overalls. Many times, especially in summer, I'd use that time to freshen up. I carried a small jar of Persil washing powder in my sugar bag, which I tied to my shovel and kept in my locker. To wash my overalls, I'd fill the cabin bucket with hot water before leaving Nantabibbie for Peecharra, sprinkle the Persil on top of the overalls, and use my hammer handle to pound the fabric. Then I'd rinse them with cold water from the tender and hang them out the side of the locomotive to let the air do its work. Meanwhile, the engineman had to concentrate on keeping the train under control on that grade by carefully manipulating the air brake.

Persil washing powder was versatile as it even cleaned a shovel nicely. At the end of a shift, I'd slightly heat my shovel blade in the firebox, wipe it with an oily rag so it would shine like new and then wash the handle (and even the broom and hammer handles) with Persil.

A shovel was a fireman's vital tool, and we'd usually stick with one particular shovel based on its weight, the quality of its blade and the thickness of its handle.

> **Some senior enginemen were very particular about their firemen keeping their shovels meticulously clean; they'd refuse to pick one up if it wasn't up to scratch.**

Each shovel was numbered and had to be picked up from the storeroom at the start of a shift and returned at the end. Some senior enginemen were very particular about their firemen keeping their shovels meticulously clean; they'd refuse to pick one up if it wasn't up to scratch. I remember Peterborough storeman Mel Rowse taking great delight when the running shift foreman sent a new fireman over to be "measured" for his first shovel. Engineman Bob Hams told of Mel's humorous antics with his tape measure. Mel would solemnly explain the importance of getting the measurement right, often asking the unsuspecting fireman to strip down to his underwear to help get an accurate reading.

The Cockburn Line

He'd then pull out his tape measure, checking arm length and the fireman's throw to ensure the shovel was the right weight.

Working on grades meant it was essential to maintain a good head of steam. Once we were away from Nackara and on the 1-in-80 grade to Peecharra, the train soon settled at a constant speed. It was then the fireman's job to keep a full head of steam with the injector nicked up just enough to let the right amount of water into the boiler to cover the steam usage. It was a section I liked to fire as I enjoyed watching the funnel clear so that another load of coal could be added to the firebox.

> **When working under full steam on a T-class locomotive, once the fire door was open I'd always shove the first full shovel of coal inside and around the fire hole door.**

When working under full steam on a T-class locomotive, once the fire door was open I'd always shove the first full shovel of coal inside and around the fire hole door. That helped keep the heat in the firebox while the door was open. Then I'd add the next two shovels, one on each side of the box, and a third down the front toward the dead plate. It was also a good idea to maintain a "heel" of coal at the back of the fire by the firebox door, a wedge-shaped fire bed with its thick end right at the door.

Even though locomotives belonged to a respective class, every single one had its own quirks. Some steamed well, while others rode rough; some were stronger than others in hauling a load; some burnt coal well while others couldn't achieve a clear funnel after adding coal; some had worn wheels and others had full-size ones. Working with steam, every mile presented a challenge. If we were unlucky enough to be on a bad steaming locomotive, we firemen tried every trick in the book to keep the steam up. It wasn't always easy, especially in extreme weather conditions. It was always a team effort. As a young fireman, I sometimes thought I was left to my own devices and wasn't

7. Peecharra – Nackara

Flues, tubes and blast pipe of a 400-class locomotive being cut up for scrap on a siding just to the west of Peterborough, November 1973. Photo: Lionel Noble.

Peterborough engineman Ken Sleep aged 83, 1974. Photo: Lionel Noble.

being observed by my mate, but I eventually learned that wasn't the case at all.

Engineman Ken Sleep once told me some of the tricks locomotive crews used to improve its steaming efficiency:

> *Old Johnston had a petticoat cowl fitted in the smoke box. It was a big bell-like piece under the funnel, but it never did a good job. I was firing for old George Meadows, trying it out on a run to Cockburn. He only got as far as Mannahill and then turned back.*
>
> *Charlie Ryan had a nozzle on the blast pipe, a smaller one that worked well. The bosses spotted it and, without a word, they put a bar across the nozzle and handed the engine over to George Miller to take to Cockburn. Old George then whacked a jimmy onto it*

The Cockburn Line

and every time he opened the regulator, it would whistle through the two jimmies.[14] *It made her steam alright!*

The blast pipe itself had a circular opening 3⅞ inches (98.4 mm) wide, set directly under the funnel in the smoke box. This pipe exhausted steam from the valves and pistons out into the atmosphere via the funnel. The effect was to heat the boiler water by drawing firebox heat, and even debris, through the boiler tubes and flues. Placing a jimmy across the orifice of the blast pipe split the steam blast and drew in more fire, supposedly boosting the locomotive's steaming qualities. The extra blast, though, caused the spark arresters to clog with cinders. It was illegal to use a jimmy since it burned extra coal, not to mention that tinkering with locomotive design was a big no-no.

> **It was illegal to use a jimmy since it burned extra coal, not to mention that tinkering with locomotive design was a big no-no.**

Quite often, when we were stopped on the loco pit after arriving at Nackara on an up movement from Methuen, there was little steam or boiler water and the firebox would be full of ash or clinker. That meant the ten minutes we were allocated for pit work was often extended, even though we did our best to work as quickly as possible. We wouldn't set off for the next climb until we'd cleaned sediment from the boiler by the operation of the blow-off cock, had a good measure of water in the boiler as shown on both gauge glasses and had built up a fire in the box strong enough to maintain steam pressure. If the pit time ran too long, the signalman would ask why and pass the details on to the train

---

[14.] A jimmy was a 15mm square bar, approximately 300mm long. One end was flattened and curved to hook onto the blast pipe nozzle, while the other end was threaded and secured with a wing nut. These tools were likely handmade in the workshops.

7. Peecharra – Nackara

controller, who'd record it on his graph. Nackara was one of those tight spots where another train always seemed to be waiting, either at Paratoo or coming down the hill from Nantabibbie. It was therefore important for the train controller to be aware of any delay so he could make the necessary changes to the service.

I was a fireman on my first trip to Cockburn with engineman Bill "Boof" Casey. Running down from Peecharra to Nackara, I could see for miles. Bill came over and said, 'See that hill over there? Looks like a big tit. At the foot of that is Yunta.' He was pointing out the large hill on the northeastern side of Yunta, the one named Tattawuppa Hill.

Another time, I was firing for Dan Brennan, heading out from Peterborough to relieve a crew coming from Cockburn who had lost a lot of time because of a poorly steaming locomotive. Knowing what they were up against, I wasn't anxious to get on

Peterborough engineman Dan Brennan, 1967.
Photo: Lionel Noble.

The Cockburn Line

board. One thing I did know was that Dan was a good man on the locomotive, and he'd find a way to make it run. He nurtured the engine as we started climbing the grade from Nackara, and before long we were making our way up the bank without any trouble at all, even making up time. The other crew had some explaining to do after their performance.

I remember Nackara as the site of a head-on collision in the late 1940s when a train from Peecharra struck a waiting train in the yard. I also recall shunting on the freight siding at Nackara when a vehicle was derailed by being pushed over the scotch block or derailer. That was my first derailment while driving. I declared at the time it wasn't my fault, but I still ended up with a docket (reprimand) for the incident.

One freezing cold day I was firing on a trip from Cockburn. It was so cold that even snow was reported in Peterborough. For some distance I had been watching a swagman getting a free ride in one of the ore trucks not too far behind the locomotive. When we stopped at McDonald's Hill, I took a flask of boiling hot tea and some biscuits back to him to warm him up. I mentioned the chap to engineman Harry Hanlon, who told me not to worry about him. But I wasn't about to let the man freeze, so I kept pestering Harry, asking if he'd let the swagman come up onto the engine for a while to warm up. Eventually Harry gave in, and

Remains of the Nackara narrow-gauge railway yard, 1973. Photo: Lionel Noble.

7. Peecharra – Nackara

I ran back at Nackara to call him over. The poor fellow could hardly make it from the truck onto the engine.

We talked as we went along, and I found out that he was a genuine case, just trying to get to Adelaide for work and to make a better life for himself. When we reached Peterborough, I arranged for him to come to my room at the YMCA (where I was boarding at the time), and he slept on the floor. Before he left, I gave him a £2 ($2.00) note in case he needed food while travelling into the city. I heard from him about a month later when he told me he was working at Holden's at Woodville. I often thought I would have liked to see him again.

T-class locomotive 258 and 400 Class locomotive 408 crossing at Nackara, 1967. 258 is on the ash pit at the end of the yard. Photo: Lionel Noble.

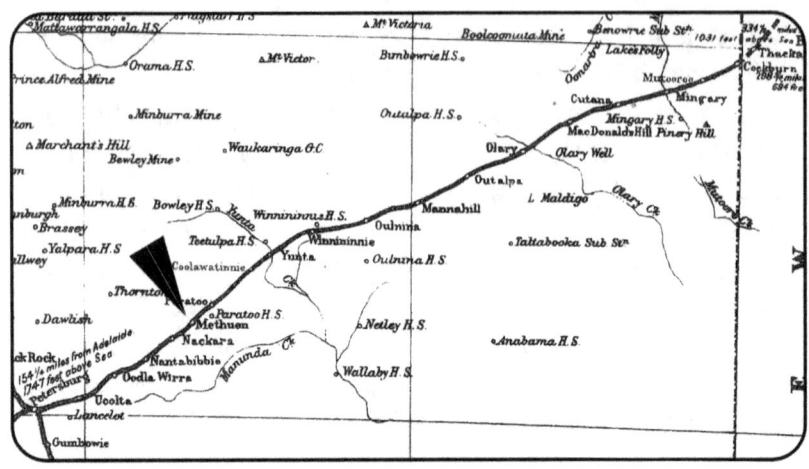

8. Nackara – Methuen

Methuen was 6¼ miles (10 km) from Nackara and 34½ miles (55.5 km) from Peterborough

According to the *Names of South Australian Railway Stations*, Methuen was named after British Lieutenant General Paul Methuen, commander of the British 1st Division in the Boer War. The section from Nackara to Methuen was a down-grade stretch, as Methuen sat only 1 133 feet (345.3 m) above sea level. Steam was needed to haul the consist out of the yard, and once the train was moving it was left to its own weight to push it down to Methuen. The down running time for freight trains was 16 minutes, while up working took 33 minutes. For up trains, pulling out of the Methuen yard meant constant shovelling for the fireman. Two level crossings were along the section, one right as you left Nackara and the other for the Broken Hill road.

In the early days, the station was a small square building with starting signal levers out the front on each side. Behind the station were weatherboard sleeping quarters, and a small metal shed was used as an oil store. Signalmen were removed on 22

8. Nackara – Methuen

May 1928, and electric staff instruments were installed and ready for use by 15 November of the same year. The station building itself was taken down in 1930.

The siding switches were first removed when the station closed in 1933. Then, due to army requirements, they were replaced in 1942, only to be removed again in 1943. Shortly thereafter, they were replaced once more, and the siding was restored for traffic in 1950 and extended another 400 feet (122 m) in 1952. The station finally closed in 1959, after having first opened back in 1889.

I remember someone once told me that when a repair was made to a railway-issued pocket watch, the details were stamped inside the rear cover so you could tally up how many times the watch had been in for repairs. One day, while we were quietly puffing our way along from Methuen to Nackara, I decided to take a closer look and unscrewed the rear cover. While I had one piece of the watch in each hand, the locomotive gauge glass burst, and I never again removed the cover of my watch!

T-class locomotives undertaking a crossing movement at Methuen. Dave Lillywhite (engineman) on T-238. Photo: Lionel Noble.

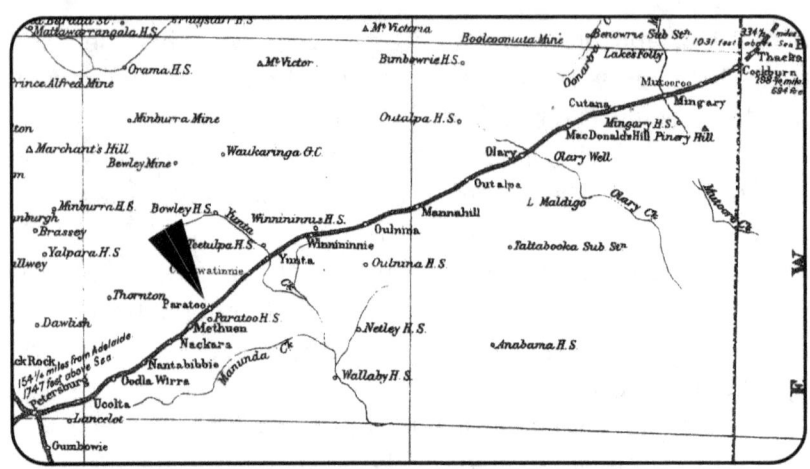

9. Methuen – Paratoo

Paratoo was 4¾ miles (7.6 km) from Methuen and 39¼ miles (63 km) from Peterborough

Paratoo sat at 995 feet (303 m) above sea level and opened to traffic in June 1886. The original station was a long wooden building, characterised by its fancy fretwork above the veranda's opening. That building was taken down in 1942 and replaced with an elevated signal cabin fitted with 18 signal/switch levers, two electric staff instruments, a party line, a train control phone and kerosene lamps. The signalman had complete control of the yard as all the yard switches were operated from the cabin by cable and steel rodding.

Only light steaming was needed from Methuen to the top of the hill at the 191-mile point before shutting off steam and running down the 1½-mile (2.4 km) grade into Paratoo. When Methuen was closed to train working, the section became simply Nackara to Paratoo. On an up movement from Paratoo, it was a 47-minute haul to Nackara that required continuous firing. With a poorly steaming locomotive, a little water could be recovered

9. Methuen – Paratoo

in the boiler along the flat or at the grade change near the 186-mile. In down running from Nackara, the running time was 27 minutes.

There was only one open level crossing on the section and that was for the original main Broken Hill road. It wasn't unusual to see kangaroos or sheep in the paddock between the line and the road, drawn in by a small windmill and trough where they could get a drink.

Back in the early days a loco pit sat at each end of the Paratoo yard. Engineman Tim Jenkins used to tell us about rabbit plagues and how he'd have to clear rabbits out of the ash pits before starting to clean the fire. Chute-type water columns also stood at each end of the yard. An overhead tank holding 25 000 gallons (113 652 L) was located near Paratoo, almost opposite the station building on the southern side. Water from the tank supplied the railway cottages and water columns. The tank itself was filled from the pump house on one of the two railway reservoirs, situated some distance up the grade toward Coolawatinnie on the left side.

A triangle to the south of the line at Paratoo was used to turn locomotives. One leg of the triangle was much longer than the

400-class locomotive 406 in the Paratoo yard, 1965. The overhead tank can be seen to the left. Photo by A. Grunbach. Used with permission of the Australian Railway Historical Society, NSW.

The Cockburn Line

The original Paratoo railway station building. Note the 'starter' signal levers at each end of the building. The starters were removed in 1924. As trains became longer in later years, signalmen used the ladder (as seen) for hand signals to the locomotive crew performing shunting duties.
Photo: Lionel Noble Collection.

The Paratoo signal cabin with the railway historical train departing, 1968.
Photo: Alex Grunbach, used with permission of the Australian Railway Historical Society, NSW.

9. Methuen – Paratoo

Paratoo signal cabin with the electric staff machine to the left, 1967.
Photo: Lionel Noble.

Signal control levers in the Paratoo narrow-gauge signal cabin, 1972.
Photo: Lionel Noble.

other, and that's where cattle were loaded and unloaded, a fair distance from the yard. The cattle ramp and the triangle were on private property, so stock roamed free. I remember the metal gate into that area often getting knocked down, bent or buckled by the locomotive cow catcher or coupling.

Paratoo station yard looking west towards Nackara, c. 1950s. The coal stage can be seen in the distance. Photo: Lionel Noble.

Apart from Cockburn, Paratoo was the only station with a coal stage. Coal was shovelled into large cane baskets that were then lifted by hand onto a higher landing and unloaded into a chute feeding the coal to the tender.[15] Members of the gang kept the baskets full, and if extra baskets were needed, the crew would fill them up. Before Paratoo had its coal stage, if locomotives ran

---

[15.] 190 baskets to one ton of coal; 185 baskets to fill a T-class tender.

9. Methuen – Paratoo

short of coal on the way from Cockburn they'd have to take coal from other locomotives on the track.

Paratoo was a reducing station and always busy; I can still recall seeing four trains there at one time.[16] William Chambers mentioned that back in those days 30 to 32 trains a day ran on the Cockburn Line, especially once they added extra trains to carry the reduced loading into Peterborough from Paratoo.

All yard movements were governed by fixed signals or hand signals shared between the guard and the signalman, who would relay them to the locomotive crew. As trains became longer in later years, shunting signals became a bit tricky, especially at the Coolawatinnie end of the yard. To help, a long ladder was propped against the side of the freight shed so a traffic employee could climb up and hand-signal the crew. This wasn't necessary in the early days because the train lengths were shorter and most vehicles in the consists were only four-wheelers.

On top of the rise before dropping down into Paratoo on a down movement, you could see the smoke from other train movements ahead and of those working home to Peterborough.

On top of the rise before dropping down into Paratoo on a down movement, you could see the smoke from other train movements ahead and of those working home to Peterborough. Likewise, a train sitting in the Paratoo yard waiting to move into the Methuen section could see the down movement coming from Methuen rounding the curve to drop down into Paratoo. When the fireman saw an approaching train, he'd start building up the fire in readiness. After the opposing train arrived and the signalman brought the Paratoo/Methuen electric staff to the locomotive and cleared the starting signal,

---

[16.] A reducing station was a location where a train's excess weight was removed before entering the next section. The offloaded weight was then picked up by a different locomotive.

the train could then enter the section toward Methuen or Nackara.

During the 1937 drought, so little water was available on the Cockburn Line that water trains had to be run to Coolawatinnie from Eurelia on the Quorn line. To avoid congesting the Paratoo yard with shunting water tanks and extra vehicles from excessive tonnage, these water trains would run to Coolawatinnie and stand on the passing siding. Tim Jenkins recalled standing at Coolawatinnie for seven hours while each up train took tanks off his train to reach Oodla Wirra. He said those were some very long hours and stirred up plenty of bad tempers.

Engineman Ken Sleep used to tell us just how difficult the water issues were.

> *No rain for many years and the drought. They put two pumps on at Paratoo ... they got the water from the Paratoo sheep station, then they put the dam on the hill at Paratoo. The water from Paratoo Station was alright but with the two pumps they got down to the sea salt [salty water]. Tubes leaking, everything was buggered. As many as four dead engines with one engine pulling them along. If it lasted another month we wouldn't have had one engine.*

I remember one occasion back in 1950 when I was driving the second locomotive on a double header. We had stopped at the water column at the eastern end of the Paratoo yard. Five railway cottages and a 12 x 12 humpy for the relief signalman were between the loco pit and the Broken Hill road. Standing on one of the cottage verandas was a fettler's wife, looking rather alarmed and pointing at the ground. We'd already started moving out of the yard when I gave two short peeps on the whistle and signalled to the leading engineman that the lady on the veranda had snake trouble. We stopped the train, grabbed our shovels, and set off after the snake. It eluded us for some time but eventually found its way into the bathroom through the bath outlet. We cornered

9. Methuen – Paratoo

it and killed it, then did our best to show Mrs Alszko that the snake was dead, but she wouldn't have any of it. Not wanting to upset her further, we ended up putting the snake in the firebox. One of the crew later joked that because the snake was black, we had black smoke all the way up the Coolawatinnie grade.

Water train at Paratoo. Tom Fitzgerald, middle on the water tank, was the author of the 1901 Walloway train accident poem. Note tenders and various tanks used for carting water. Photo: Lionel Noble Collection.

Paratoo railway yard and cottages looking towards Nackara, 1967. Photo: Alex Grunbach, used with permission of the Australian Railway Historical Society, NSW.

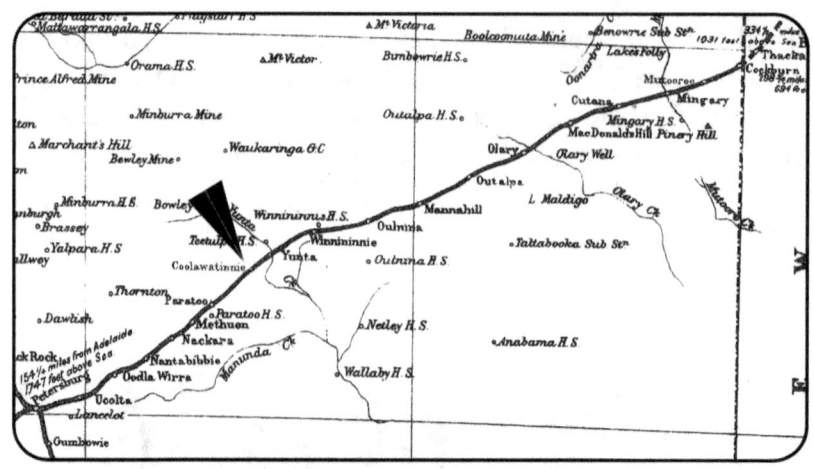

10. Paratoo – Coolawatinnie

Coolawatinnie was 5¼ miles (8.5 km) from Paratoo and 44½ miles (71.6 km) from Peterborough

The Coolawatinnie station, located at the 198¾-mile marker, stood at 1 153 feet (351.5 m) above sea level. It was opened in October 1928 and closed in 1959. Being an unattended station, it was later closed as a block station for electric staff working on 5 August 1934. The grade out of Paratoo dipped toward a watercourse crossed by a large bridge, and from that point there was a gradual, nearly straight climb to Coolawatinnie. The climb changed slightly toward the top as it curved to the left before going straight again into the Coolawatinnie yard. Scheduled running time was 23 minutes on a down movement and 16 minutes on an up run. Arriving at Coolawatinnie, you could see for miles ahead and behind the train.

    Two level crossings were along this section. The first, right as you left the Paratoo yard, was the main crossing for those travelling to or from the Paratoo sheep station. The second was rarely used but also provided access to the sheep station. That

10. Paratoo – Coolawatinnie

spot was where the tucker train dropped off chaff when the reservoirs were being cleaned out by horse teams, and it was also where coal was dumped onto a ground-level platform built of sleepers. The coal then went on to fuel the pump house and supply the pumper who lived at Paratoo.

It was very near the second crossing that 400-class locomotive 408 rolled over at 1.45 am on 27 December 1960 near the 196-mile marker, caused by a heat buckle in the line. The movement was the 222 up Broken Hill express and engineman Harry Viney was killed in the accident. The locomotive rolled onto its left side and, in so doing, scraped the ground as it moved forward; the cabin filled with dirt, and Harry suffocated as soil filled his mouth. After the derailment, fireman Ron Kamin and guard Bruce McPherson couldn't locate Harry, until they eventually noticed fingers protruding from a mound of dirt in the cabin. Harry was an Englishman whose only relative was his mother, still living in England. The oil patch that spilled from the locomotive's tank could be seen for years afterwards. It was a sad business.

> **The locomotive rolled onto its left side and, in so doing, scraped the ground as it moved forward; the cabin filled with dirt, and Harry suffocated as soil filled his mouth.**

The hill where Coolawatinnie was situated is known as Dead Man's Hill because of the large white wooden cross next to the track at the back of the station. George Miller told me that the person buried there was on his way to make his money at the Waukaringa gold mines. The body had been found further down the hill toward Paratoo, near an early-day's eating house. William Chambers, who was once stationed at Coolawatinnie, was in his 90s when he related the story of that cross as told to him by Micky Coglin.

A mailman used to drive the mail through, I think it was from Burra to the Waukaringa gold mines, before the

The Cockburn Line

The cross marking the grave at Dead Man's Hill at Coolawatinnie, c. 1970s. Photo: Lionel Noble.

railway was built to Cockburn. He then used to move on about 2 miles from the Paratoo sheep station and take his horses out and camp. One night he died and was buried at the foot of a sandalwood tree. Les Clayson and I found the grave, formed it up and I made a cross and put it at the head of the grave and painted the cross white. I tried through the police at Yunta to find out the man's name, but all I was told was that he was an Irishman. We found the grave in 1911 and tended it until 1922 when I left the north.

Chambers and members of the gang at Coolawatinnie erected that cross during their time as gangers. Every time the railway

10. Paratoo – Coolawatinnie

painters came through the area, they'd repaint the cross, and it could be seen for quite a distance.

Over the years, many rabbit plagues swept along the Cockburn Line and I remember seeing thousands of them around Coolawatinnie. Away from the line, hundreds would sit on warrens, while those closer would scatter like flies. At other times, kangaroos were as common as sheep in the paddocks. I recall two incidents with them. Once, while firing and travelling from Paratoo to Coolawatinnie, a large red kangaroo jumped beside us inside the railway fence, keeping pace with the train for a considerable distance. I watched to see how far it would go when suddenly it turned and, with its head down, jumped straight into the side of our locomotive. The driving connecting rod hit it, and that was that.

Another time, as we were running down from Coolawatinnie to Paratoo, we found ourselves pacing a blue doe kangaroo at around 25–30 mph (40–48 kph). The speed of these smaller animals was amazing. While I was watching it in flight, she suddenly tossed out her joey and kept going, then just as suddenly stopped, turned, and went in the opposite direction. They say that when danger prevails, a kangaroo will go back for its joey once the threat has passed.

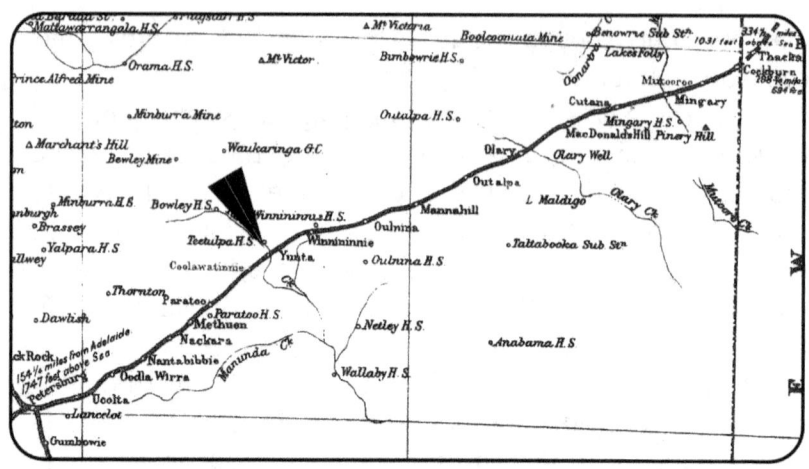

11. Coolawatinnie – Yunta

Yunta was 8¼ miles (13.3 km) from Coolawatinnie and 52¾ miles (85 km) from Peterborough

Multiple explanations exist for the origin of the name Yunta. The South Australian Railways book on railway names says that the word "has reference to the anatomy of a woman". Mr Coombe of the SA Museum said, "To the tribes of Lake Eyre the word meant a bull roarer, that is, a piece of wood attached to a string of human hair which, when swung rapidly with a circular motion, produced a penetrating sound." To the Dieri mob, the word "Yuntha" meant a certain piece of wood used in ceremonial dances. Lutheran missionary, Pastor Schurmann, recorded the words "Yanta" and "Yarnta" as meaning "there" or "at a place". Pastor Meyer described the word "Yunte" as meaning "together" or "to assemble". Professor NB Tindale said the word was derived from the indigenous word "Junta" (pronounced Yu-nta) meaning female genital organs. Horace Cobden Talbot agrees, saying Yunta is "modestly defined as referring to a woman's anatomy". The jury is still out!

11. Coolawatinnie – Yunta

*The Yunta railway station and goods shed, 1947.
Stationmaster Ian O'Brien's son in front of the office.
Photos: Lionel Noble Collection.*

The Cockburn Line

Yunta sat at 992 feet (302 m) above sea level, and the station yard was level. It was a very busy station: wool, stock, sheep, sandalwood and ballast were trucked away (the sandalwood to China and the ballast throughout the Division). To accommodate all the freight, they built a large, dome-roofed freight shed that also housed the station office. A 5-ton crane was positioned on the freight platform at the Paratoo end of the shed. I recall 1951 being a busy year as on one day in April 57 vehicles of up-loading were on hand. Yard congestion was common.

The emergency overhead oil tanks at Yunta for locomotive use. The railway cottages (demolished 1990) are of an unusual design which was also used at Nackara and Gladstone. Photo: Lionel Noble.

On the Paratoo side of the station was a 25 000-gallon (94 635 L) overhead tank, two signalman's cottages, the stationmaster's house and a shed housing the generator for the town and railway power supply. On the Winnininnie end were sheep and cattle yards, loading ramps and a freight spur which, in the early days, went down into the large Yunta Creek where ballast was loaded into Z-class hoppers. Wool was loaded into trucks at the freight platform, and on the other side of the up main line were six plain-looking cottages, all a reasonable size. The post office

11. Coolawatinnie – Yunta

Early type railway employee cottages similar to those on the Cockburn line at Yunta, c. 1910s. Photo: Lionel Noble Collection.

building was originally in the railway yard by the gates on the main street but was later moved to Waukaringa.

On a down movement, steam was usually needed to lift the train out of the Coolawatinnie yard around the curve toward Yunta. The train would then run down a straight line for several miles until about two miles from Yunta, then along a level stretch, followed by light steaming into Yunta station. The scheduled time for the section was 20 minutes for down trains and 32 minutes for up working. Up working from Yunta began with light steaming and then all shovelling for the fireman.

Two level crossings were along the section. The first was about halfway down the hill, and the second, used extensively by vehicles travelling to and from several large sheep properties south of the line, was between fixed signals very close to the Yunta yard.

When heavy rains came, the lower end of the section near Yunta was prone to flooding. Water runoff from the lower Paratoo side passed under a large bridge and, at the Yunta end, floodwaters from the hills of Coolawatinnie flowed through several small

The Cockburn Line

culverts that weren't sufficient during heavy rains. As a result, water often spilled over the line, washing out the ballast and causing train delays. It was a frightful sight to see swirling floodwaters on both sides of the locomotive, and many times the engineman had to decide whether to press on or stay put.

I remember one night at 2.00 am when I was the engineman on a 300-class Garratt locomotive running down from Coolawatinnie. About two miles out from Yunta, I heard loud banging and saw sparks coming from the side of the locomotive. When I stopped the train, I found that one unit connecting rod had uncoupled from the piston rod at the crosshead and was lying on the ground. We were at the 205½-mile marker and stranded with no communications. At that hour, our guard Trixie Munro wasn't very interested—or interesting! With that class of locomotive, you always expected something to go wrong.

I assessed the situation and sent my fireman, W Kuester, off with a note for the porter in charge at Yunta station, advising him of what had happened. I told him I'd arrive as soon as repairs were finished. To help me see what I was doing, I lit a huge fire topped with sleepers, which kept me warm and at the same time lit up half of Australia.

A defect like that meant I had to pull down the side of the locomotive. The job involved removing the connecting rod (or what was left of it), disconnecting the eccentric rod and combination lever from the radius rod, and securing both the valve and piston crossheads to prevent any movement. It had only been the previous week that acting instructor Tim Jenkins showed me how to use a new clamp for the valve spindle. I hauled it out ready for use but couldn't remember how to operate it. Looking around for something I could cobble together as a fix, I went over to the railway fence, cut off some of Mr McDonald's fence wire, and set about securing the crosshead using a cross stitch of plain and purl. I then hoisted the bent pieces up onto the footplate (a feat, apparently), made a steam test and, without waiting for my fireman, eventually made it into Yunta. All went well.

11. Coolawatinnie – Yunta

When we finally arrived in Cockburn in daylight, we were met by the loco foreman. I suggested he remove the wire and put the clamp on. 'Bugger it,' was his reply. 'If it can come all the way from Yunta, the bloody thing can go home just fine.' And so it did, all thanks to Mr McDonald's fencing wire. That was the kind of thing an engineman was expected to do to at least get the train off the section.

400-class locomotive 409 taking on water in the Yunta yard, 2 April 1961. Photo: Lionel Noble.

Mrs McSomebody's bull often roamed the Yunta yard. When a stock train was standing in the yard en route to Peterborough, the bull would go completely bonkers, bellowing and stomping up and down the length of the train. One day I was firing for Archie Williams and we were carrying out our normal loco pit work. Arch was oiling the slide bars by the smoke box, and I was up on the tender adding water from the column. I spotted the bull on the other side of some ballast hoppers. I can make a realistic noise like a cow, which I did. Upon hearing the cow noise, the bull immediately responded by racing around the ballast hoppers toward Archie. Since he didn't see the animal coming, I sensed disaster, so I yelled and pointed. Poor old Arch did one spring straight off the ground onto the footplate just as the bull

The Cockburn Line

shot past him. I still see his white face shouting something like, 'You bloody idiot!' Archie only had two legs, but the bull didn't care at that stage and was after him for sure.[17]

On another occasion, Max Twigden was firing for engineman George Blyth, and they were on the loco pit at Yunta. Max was cleaning the fire and preparing it for the next section. George was on the ground examining the locomotive and picking up pieces of coal he found, placing them on the tender flap (the curved piece of metal covering the floor space between the tender and the cabin). In the interest of nothing going to waste, George expected Max to toss the pieces onto the tender. Max, however, threw them straight out the other side of the cabin. While continuing his examination, George eventually made his way around to the other side, where he was no doubt pleased to see more coal he could salvage, some of which he'd previously placed on the flap. Max then threw them out again, back to the side from which they'd originated!

Peterborough Loco Inspector Archie Williams, c. 1960s. Photo: Lionel Noble.

Peterborough engineman Max Twigden, September 1969. Photo: Lionel Noble.

[17.] Editor's note: Dad's cow call was virtually indistinguishable from a real cow. I recall driving in the countryside on one occasion when we stopped beside a paddock with grazing cows. Dad stepped out and mimicked the cow sound near the fence which startled the cows so much that they literally jumped and started running en mass toward Dad. It was quite a sight.

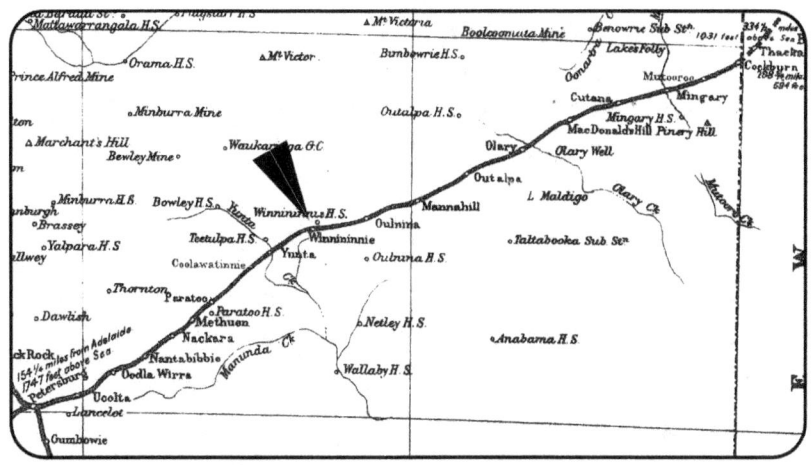

12. Yunta – Winnininnie

Winnininnie was 9¼ miles (15 km) from Yunta and 62 miles (99.8 km) from Peterborough

Winnininnie stood 1 106 feet (337 m) above sea level. The siding opened for traffic on 14 June 1887 and closed on 30 June 1963. The name, a native word meaning "much", "many" or "a gathering place", was applied by J Hallet to his pastoral property around 1856.

At one time, the Winnininnie siding was a busy place. There were railway cottages, a wooden station building, a small supply shed, a freight platform and yards for sheep and cattle. With the large Winnininnie sheep station nearby, even boasting a government gaol on its property, the yards were well patronised. It was a scenic part of the Cockburn trip; hills surrounded the route, and the line's profile—up, slight down, then near level—forced the train to change speeds and, with it, altered the rhythm of the funnel's exhaust beat.

The section heading to Winnininnie began just past the up distant signal and over the large Yunta Creek bridge. After

The Cockburn Line

that, a gradual grade lifted the train to the 209¾-mile marker, where steam was shut off until the 212½-mile point, just before crossing the large Warrawarumbie Creek. From there, it was back to shovelling our way to Winnininnie. Only two level crossings were on the section, both running into private land.

Winnininnie station and employee cottages, October 1965. Photo: Dean Harvey Collection, National Railway Museum, Port Adelaide (199-1201-b38-04)

That part of the Cockburn Line was straightforward for a fireman, provided you had good coal and a well-steaming locomotive. Keeping the engine steaming wasn't a matter of just hurling coal into the firebox; it had to be placed just right for the most efficient burn. A quick glance at the steam pressure gauge and boiler water level would reveal if things hadn't been laid in properly.

My job as a fireman was a challenge from the moment I climbed aboard until I signed off at the end of my run. Maintaining steady steam pressure, the proper water level, keeping the boiler free of sediment and keeping the cabin and tools clean—all while staying alert—demanded time, thought and energy. I always said a fireman spent half his time staring at the funnel and the firebox; those two spots told you whether the locomotive was being fired properly. It felt great and I loved it, especially once I started driving.

12. Yunta – Winnininnie

Western Endeavour historical train across Australia at the Winnininnie yard, 1970. Photo: M Billett.

Many enginemen would give the fireman a spell between Yunta and Winnininnie. As soon as the train left the station, the engineman would assume my fireman's duties while I sat in the engineman's seat, keeping a sharp lookout for any anomalies and, sometimes, nibbling on a sandwich. If a fireman held an air brake certificate, some enginemen would even let him drive. Others preferred that the fireman know the running time so the train stayed on schedule while he kept the fire going. Younger enginemen would sometimes let the fireman adjust the reversing gear lever when the train was picking up or losing speed on the grade, but they'd never allow him to stop the train. A fireman's brief drive usually ended at the distant signal, but it at least gave him a break from shovelling, even if it meant cleaning up the engineman's mess afterwards.

During summer, it was the fireman's duty to keep the tucker boxes cool, which meant keeping wet the wheat bags covering each box. When the mercury hit 115° F (46.1° C) for days on end, there wasn't much chance of stopping the butter from turning into liquid, though every bit helped. To keep coal dust from swirling into the cabin, we'd douse the coal on the tender with buckets of water. A hand bucket, kept full from a small tap under the tucker box trays right behind the driver's seat, and a hand

The Cockburn Line

broom dipped in water and flicked across the floor, were our best defences against the dust.

Some of the older enginemen had their quirks. I remember one man would shuffle his feet if there was even the smallest bit of coal underneath. One day a fireman, having a particularly rough day, grew annoyed by this habit; he lobbed a generous shovel of coal at his mate's feet while calling out, 'Scratch in that, you old fowl!'

On 24 February 1939, Warrawarumbie Creek was in flood, with water rising 2 feet (61 cm) above the main Broken Hill road bridge opposite the rail line. Whenever I passed that section, I couldn't help but recall the old bullockies' tales of their teams getting bogged down. They'd boast that their animals were so strong, they could even shift the bed of the creek when hauling out a load.

> **I heard an unusual noise coming from just beneath the locomotive cabin, a noise that seemed to be linked to a wheel.**

I had two breakdowns on that part of the track, both at the Yunta end and both while I was an engineman. One time, we were working a produce train with a 400-class locomotive in one of those all-the-way movements (they always said 'all gates opened'). We'd departed Yunta at about 1.00 am. A while after crossing the Yunta Creek bridge, I heard an unusual noise coming from just beneath the locomotive cabin, a noise that seemed to be linked to a wheel. I stopped the train off the bridge to investigate the small pony wheel on my side. Carefully running my hand around its rim, I discovered a buildup of metal at one spot, a sure sign that the axle had stopped turning at some point while we were still in motion. Oddly, only one pony wheel was affected.

After arranging with the guard and station porter to return to Yunta, I noticed the axle still wasn't rotating during our reverse journey. This defect was unlike anything I'd seen before, so I sought out the loco superintendent at the time, Ken Bettison. He

12. Yunta – Winnininnie

The heavy duty jacks on a 400-class locomotive, usually used for re-railing. This locomotive was being cut up for scrap in Peterborough, November 1973. Photo: Lionel Noble.

instructed me on what to do next. The repair job called for taking the weight off the pony wheels using the two jacks stowed in the "duck pond" of the locomotive.

The work dragged on for several hours and had to be completed in darkness. By the end, we'd been on duty for nearly nine hours and were dead tired. The final task was to reposition the jacks in the duck pond, a process that took us much longer than lowering them in the first place. As I set the last jack in place, I remarked to my mate, 'If he (meaning Ken Bettison) wants them down again, he can get them down himself.'

No sooner had I said that than I heard a voice behind me asking, 'You wouldn't be that hard on me, would you?' It turned out to be Ken, who had driven out from Peterborough to check that all was well.

From Yunta, we returned to Peterborough light locomotive running at various speeds.[18] I still remember Mr Bettison

---

[18.] "Running light locomotive" referred to a locomotive operating on its own, without any attached load.

The Cockburn Line

pouring water over a wheel to keep its rim wet whenever it touched the rail, preventing sparks and potential damage.

At Peterborough, the pony wheels were removed, dismantled and examined, yet no fault was found with the bearings. They even weighed the locomotive on the depot's weighbridge to check for any imbalance, but everything appeared normal, and we never did figure out why that axle wouldn't rotate. It never came under notice again.

The other breakdown I experienced occurred near the 210-mile post. That day, I was on a T-class locomotive hauling a fully loaded ore train from Cockburn. My fireman, King Winkworth, alerted me to a knocking and smoking condition on his side of the locomotive. I walked onto the footplate and noticed that part of the top shoe of the crosshead was missing. I stopped the train for a closer look and discovered that one back top slide bar bolt was missing. Clearly, the bolt had come loose and dropped, striking the top crosshead shoe and leaving only a small remnant as a guide. Something had to be done.

With a T-class, or with any steam locomotive, a job like that could take several hours.

Since we were near the top of the grade just before descending into Yunta station, we decided to press on slowly to Yunta where we could pull down the side of the locomotive. In simple terms, that meant removing the connecting rod, disconnecting the valve rod, and securing both the piston crosshead and the valve spindle rod. Luckily, Yunta had two loco pits, and having access to one made the job much easier. Without a pit, there'd have been barely enough room to move, let alone work.

I recall King saying he was extremely interested in the whole affair as it was his first breakdown. Freshly discharged after many years in the Royal Australian Navy during the war, he hadn't been firing for long but proved as keen as mustard and a real asset on the locomotive. I explained to him exactly what needed to be done and how we were going to do it.

12. Yunta – Winnininnie

With a T-class, or with any steam locomotive, a job like that could take several hours. Once we got started, I didn't fancy running up and down checking the boiler water level and fire condition every five minutes. So, before we began, we filled the boiler, loaded a good heap of coal inside the firebox door, set the steam pressure to about 160 psi and closed the circulatory jet. The locomotive had to be positioned so that the gudgeon pin in the crosshead could be removed. We went back and forth a few times until we got it just right. I then went to climb underneath to start the work and, to my dismay, discovered we weren't aligned properly over the pit! We had to begin the alignment process all over again. Lesson number one: take everything into consideration.

In the steam days on the Peterborough division there was a great comradeship among the men. Every man pitched in and worked hard for the betterment of their job. Trains ran on time

Winnininnie railway station, c. 1950s. Left, Lionel Noble (engineman), right Victor Hawes (guard) with the 'thunder box' to the rear. Photo: Lionel Noble Collection.

and the crews did their utmost to see that everything came together harmoniously. Part of that camaraderie was expressed in the pranks we played on one another. During the summer months, we firemen would do our best to toss a bucket of water over a mate on a passing train. The fun, as we called it, was shared only among us firemen and most of the time the enginemen didn't mind. We just had to pick our mark carefully, as a few enginemen never saw the funny side of things.

Our team included Max Twigden, John Wills, Ken Saint, Dave Lillywhite and Lloyd Chamberlayne. We'd spend time studying the roster so we could catch one another off guard with the water. One day I'd worked out that John Wills, my brother-in-law, was scheduled on the train we were set to cross at Winnininnie. As his locomotive passed, I tossed a bucket into the cab expecting to drench John, only to find that King Winkworth was sitting in the seat. All I could see after their train came to a stop was a figure stomping down the yard in my direction. I was certain my block was about to be knocked off but, since the train spanned the full length of the yard, King had time to cool off. His main concern was his damp tobacco and it cost me two ounces' worth of roll-your-own tobacco and papers.

> **The other man tried to return the favour but ended up falling off the locomotive onto the embankment. He managed to clamber back onto the train's guard van as it rolled past.**

On another occasion, I filled a bucket with water and threw it at the fireman on a passing train. The other man tried to return the favour but ended up falling off the locomotive onto the embankment. He managed to clamber back onto the train's guard van as it rolled past.

Once, when my fireman had dozed off on his seat, I decided to teach him a lesson by climbing out of the cabin onto the roof. He got quite a fright when he woke up, thinking I'd fallen off the

12. Yunta – Winnininnie

train. And then there were the weightlifting competitions, which I always lost. Determined to get my own back, I challenged one of the other drivers to try lifting me. He failed to realise that I'd hooked my belt through a handrail and he nearly lifted the whole train trying to hoist me up!

*Oil-burning T-class locomotive 51, a familiar sight on the Cockburn Line in the steam era.
Photo: Lionel Noble.*

The Cockburn Line

Oulnina railway station and signal cabin, c. 1950s. Photos: Lionel Noble.

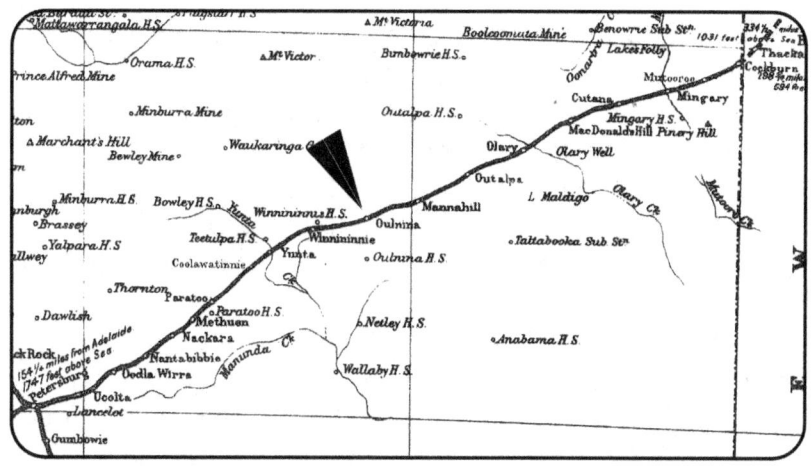

13. Winnininnie – Oulnina

Oulnina was 8¾ miles (14 km) from Winnininnie and 70¾ miles (114.9 km) from Peterborough

The Oulnina siding, located at the 225-mile mark, stood 1 425 feet (434 m) above sea level. According to Manning, the name was first applied to a pastoral lease in 1857 and meant "good water". The siding opened in 1888 and closed in 1963. This section was the heaviest between Yunta and Cockburn, being a climb of 319 feet (97.2 m). When working down, we had to steam hard almost all the way since the grade started right at the switches at Winnininnie. The scheduled running time for freight movements was 30 minutes in the down direction and 23 minutes when working up. On the up trip we enjoyed an entire down grade, which meant no steaming was needed.

Two level crossings were along this stretch. The first was an occupational crossing near a bore and tank at the 220-mile peg. The bore, on the right-hand side of the line, was 201 feet (61.3 m) deep and produced salty water. The second crossing, near the 223-mile post, was used only occasionally.

The Cockburn Line

The area was prone to flooding because water from nearby hills on the south side of the track often caused delays. Even the lightest thundery shower could wash away ballast along the line. Two creeks were in the area: one at the 221-mile 37-chain mark, known as Pine Creek or Well Paddock Creek, and a shallow creek at the 222-mile marker. Eventually, all the water found its way onto the plains and then into Warrawarumbie Creek at the 213-mile mark.

To me, Oulnina was about halfway to Cockburn. It was a siding where we usually got a 15-minute meal break, no matter which direction we were headed. The moment the train stopped, a crow would take flight from the scrub and settle on the tender, waiting patiently to be fed by the crew.

Oulnina was also where my long-time fireman, Cliff "Nugget" Sleep, would lean over an open underground tank hole looking for any trapped snakes. If he spotted one, he'd swiftly pour a bucket of hot water on it and then use his long fire pricker to pluck it out. On an up movement, he'd hold onto the snake until we reached Winnininnie and then he'd wind it around the electric staff hoop and hand it over to the young porter at Yunta. It was amusing to watch how quickly that white-faced porter dropped the hoop! By then, the snake was long cooked, dead from having been boiled two stations back.

Tom Fitzgerald used to tell a story about Alf Dickson, who fired for him back in the early days. Alf was a classy runner who stayed in shape by hopping off the locomotive and running alongside the train for a mile or so. Tom also recalled a tale about Jack Hambly, from his time at Oulnina around 1900. One early morning in the Oulnina office, Jack was busy on his knees scrubbing the floor

13. Winnininnie – Oulnina

when he suddenly sensed he wasn't alone. Looking up, he found a bullock peering down at him, evidently interested in the water in his bucket. Wasting no time, Jack crawled under the beast's body and roused his mate. Manoeuvring to back the unwelcome visitor into the passage, and not straight through the door, required quite clever wrangling.

Jack was the first signalman on the Cockburn Line to face the problem of overlapping trains. The issue arose when two long trains arrived at Oulnina at the same time, each one longer than the yard could hold. For years, seasoned enginemen would give a new chum a hard time about coming up with a solution to that very problem. I remember engineman Fred Eckert, who relished those challenges, asking me exactly that. The solution went like this:

- Train No. 1 would arrive in the yard and stop at the fouling point. From that position, one could count how many vehicles extended beyond the fouling peg at the rear.
- Knowing that number, the whole train was reversed, and the excess vehicles were detached onto the main line.
- With the train now clear at both ends, it pulled into the yard.
- When Train No. 2 arrived, it was admitted onto the clear line, passed through the yard, and coupled with the excess vehicles left on the main line, ensuring its rear was in the clear.
- Next, Train No. 1 pulled ahead as far as the distant signal or yard limit board and stopped.
- Then, Train No. 2 reversed back into the yard with the excess vehicles attached at the front of its locomotive.
- Once in a clear spot, those excess vehicles were uncoupled, and Train No. 2 continued toward the rear of Train No. 1.
- When Train No. 2 was free of the facing switches, it pulled ahead and left the station.
- Finally, Train No. 1 reversed to pick up the excess vehicles, re-coupled, and was ready to depart.

The Cockburn Line

Throughout the whole manoeuvre, Train No. 2 remained coupled. In later years, train controllers would avoid the hassle entirely by simply knowing the exact length of each train. Things were a little different in those early days.

Then there was one late evening at Oulnina. I was on a freight train standing on the passing siding with Cliff Sleep as my fireman. We were delayed for some reason, so we shut down our 400-class locomotive. From Oulnina, you could see the lights of Mannahill and those of an oncoming opposing train. That meant we had just enough time to build up the steam pressure before the other train arrived. It was a balmy, windless night. Cliff always carried a fox whistle, which he'd made from the lid of a condensed milk can. We sat quietly, and every so often he'd blow the whistle. The foxes, always curious, would appear; it was amazing to see their eyes catch the beam of a torchlight. Those cunning creatures would move in a semi-circle around us, though never venturing too close to the locomotive from where the sound came.

300-class locomotive at Oulnina on 226 up, 6 September 1952.
Photo: Lionel Noble Collection.

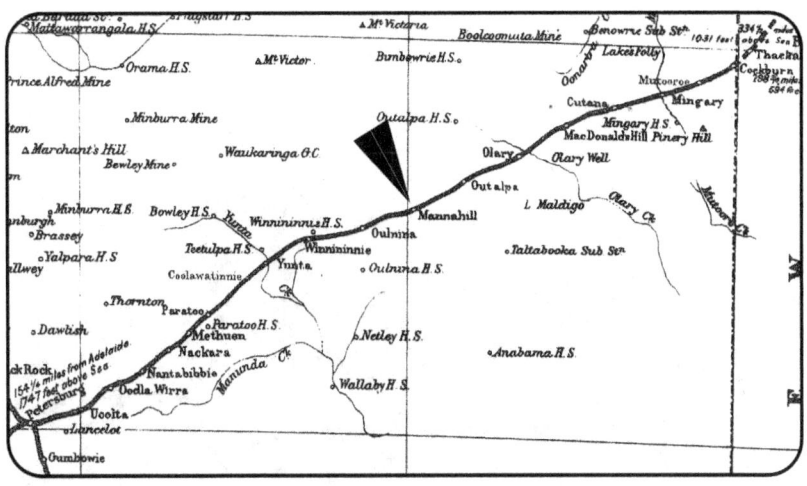

14. Oulnina – Mannahill

Mannahill was 9 miles (14.5 km) from Oulnina and 79¾ miles (128.3 km) from Peterborough

When looking towards Mannahill from Oulnina, Oulnina seemed to be so much higher, but the difference was only 209 feet (63.7 m) with Mannahill standing at 1 216 feet (370.6 m) above sea level. Mannahill was a facetious name given by shearers to the area around an old eating house. The siding opened for rail traffic on 14 June 1887 and, at first, it was simply a siding with a train examiner checking the trains bound for and coming from Cockburn. Toward the end of the narrow-gauge era, the Mannahill station was closed for train operations and became unattended on 1 November 1968.

On the run from Oulnina to Mannahill there was only a short stretch where light steaming was required. For the rest of the way, the train would coast up to the reservoir bridge just outside the Mannahill signals. The schedule called for 23 minutes on the down run and 35 minutes, all steaming, on the up. Only one level crossing was along this stretch, located near the railway

The Cockburn Line

*Mannahill station and railway yard, 1987.
The station closed on 1 November 1987.
Photo: Lionel Noble.*

reservoirs about 1½ miles (2.4 km) from the Mannahill yard. The line also crossed two large creeks with pleasant names: Jacobs and Jumbuck creeks.

The original Mannahill station was a timber structure comprising a living room, office, waiting shed, porter's room, ladies' room, men's toilet and a camp room. The porter's and ladies' rooms were closed in 1960. In the mid-1930s, the refreshment rooms—housed in a substantial stone building—were re-purposed into offices and the stationmaster's residence.

During my time working on the line, the ladies of Mannahill would prepare light meals for passengers aboard the Broken Hill Christmas picnic trains, raising funds for local projects. The trains stopped at Mannahill for loco requirements, giving passengers time to grab a bite and a drink. Typically, two such trains ran each Friday night, spaced about an hour apart. After a month away, passengers returned to Broken Hill aboard the same trains, departing Adelaide on Friday evenings.

14. Oulnina – Mannahill

Early Mannahill railway station prior to construction of the stone building, c. 1900. Photo: Lionel Noble Collection.

New Mannahill refreshment rooms and railway station, c. 1940s. Photo: Lionel Noble Collection.

The Cockburn Line

In 1925 a telephone was installed in the station for communicating with the 244-mile mark near Outalpa and at the 244-mile 70-chain. That phone was used to warn the station when heavy dust storms threatened to stop a train making headway. I remember my first encounter with one such storm when I was firing for engineman Dan Brennan on the tucker train. The dust was so thick on our run from Oulnina to Mannahill that we couldn't even see the fences, let alone much else. It was a strange sight: the locomotive lights on a little after lunch and Dan periodically blowing the whistle into the dusty gloom.

Mannahill railway siding and railway employee cottages, 1987.
Photo: Lionel Noble.

Colin Hocking lived in a modest cottage at the Outalpa end of the yard. In his front yard, he'd hoisted what looked like the frame of an iron double bed, re-purposed as a television antenna. Colin was, by all accounts, the first person in Mannahill to own a television. He pieced together a six-inch receiver using parts scrounged from disposal shops scattered across every state. At that end of the yard stood two signalmen's cottages and

14. Oulnina – Mannahill

two loco cottages, in front of which had once stood a weatherboard building, though it was removed as early as 1902. These cottages sat directly opposite the first facing switches at the Outalpa end at the 234-mile 9-chain mark.

A 400-class locomotive departing Mannahill from the Oulnina end of the yard, c. 1960s. Cattle loading ramps to the right. Photo: Lionel Noble.

400-class locomotive 403 in the Mannahill yard, 1950. L to R: Joe Jedrich (fireman), Dave Lillywhite (engineman) and Fred Matthews (guard). Photo: Lionel Noble.

The Cockburn Line

A horse yard had been built alongside the cottages on the station side. There were also temporary barracks at one time: a double wood and iron cottage on the street side, with one room specifically reserved for railway crews.

Many years back I was working a stock train from Mannahill with fireman Paul Diamantis. We'd travelled with our locomotive and brake van from Peterborough, only to run into trouble loading the cattle. In the end, we had to spend the night at the Mannahill Hotel because the cattle just wouldn't budge.

T-class locomotive 242 passing through the Mannahill yard at night. Note the engineman dropping off the electric staff hoop. Photo: Lionel Noble.

Mannahill had two reservoirs of good capacity, draining a large catchment area. After heavy rains you could see the expanse of water running down the hill from Oulnina. All the drains off the hills and creeks were directed to the catchment area. When the reservoirs ran dry, water trains were hauled in from Eurelia and Hall's Well on the Quorn line using ballast hoppers converted to carry water. Engineman Joe Harding used to say that water trains could take as long as 16 hours to run

14. Oulnina – Mannahill

from Peterborough to Mannahill. He'd laugh and add that you could stand a spoon on its end in the water from Hall's Well. That poor quality water adversely affected the locomotive boilers; sometimes there'd be as many as a dozen boilermakers on a shift at Peterborough just to keep them in working order.

I remember there were years when rabbits were everywhere on this section. Sometimes there were thousands hopping about in the paddocks on the right, between the 227- and 229-mile marks, all inside the railway fence.

It was on that same section on the way to Cockburn that I once had a broken eccentric strap, just after rounding the curve at the 226¾-mile mark. And as usual, it happened under cover of darkness. Fixing that type of defect required a procedure much like pulling down the side of a T-class locomotive, except on that occasion I didn't have a loco pit to work with.

In 1965, I recall engineman Tom Whitford having several trucks derail at the rear of his train on the Oulnina side of the distant signal as he entered the Mannahill yard. It turned out a broken truck axle was to blame. Then there was engineman JJ Reynolds, whose six-wheel loaded water tank derailed and caused track damage stretching for many miles. While repairs were underway, trains had to move over the affected area at just 10 mph (16.1 kph), which significantly added to the running time on that section.

Derailment on the Cockburn line at the 234-mile entering Mannahill, 1965. Photo: Lionel Noble.

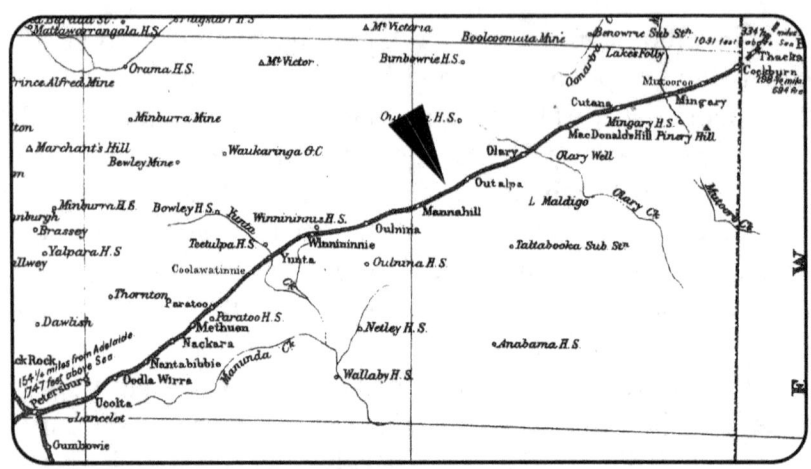

15. Mannahill – Wawirra

Wawirra was 5¾ miles (9.3 km) from Mannahill and 85½ miles (137.6 km) from Peterborough

Wawirra got its name from a local pastoral lease, and the yard stood at 1 070 feet (326 m) above sea level. Like other intermediate stops on the Cockburn Line, Wawirra was opened, closed and reopened. It first opened on 2 November 1928 and finally closed in 1959. No railway houses were there, just the usual humpy on the south of the main line complete with electric staff instruments and phones.

For the fireman on a down movement, two fires were enough between Mannahill and Wawirra. We'd run light steaming for the first two miles from Mannahill and then, after rounding a curve, the train would coast down a 1-in-120 grade to Wawirra. On an up journey, heavy steaming was needed until we reached the Mannahill distant signal. The scheduled running time for the section was 14 minutes for the down run and 27 minutes for the up. Two lines were in the yard, the main line and the passing siding, and the only road

15. Mannahill – Wawirra

crossing was right after leaving the Mannahill yard, between the signals.

The main Broken Hill road ran along the left, as did a small airfield for light aircraft. Off to the right, a large hill stood out on the horizon. I remember on up movements, old drivers pointing out that when that hill was straight to your left, you were headed into Mannahill.

830-class locomotive 867 on the Wawirra narrow-gauge bridge, 1967.
Photo: Lionel Noble.

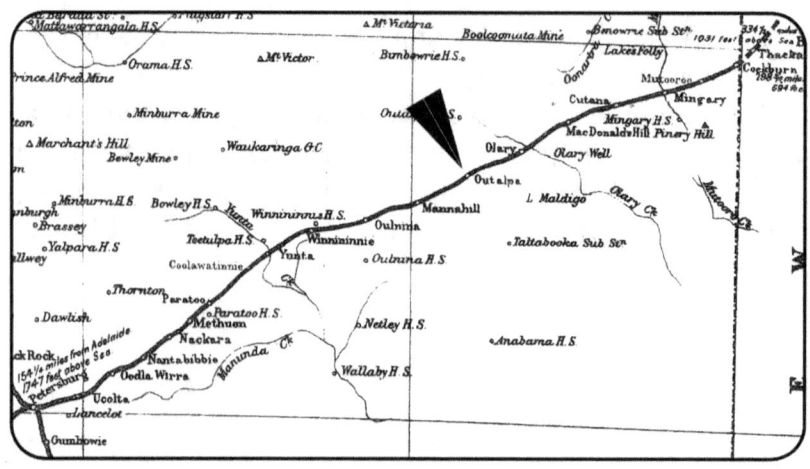

16. Wawirra – Outalpa

Outalpa was 6¾ miles (10.9 km) from Wawirra and 85½ miles (137.6 km) from Peterborough

Outalpa yard sat at the 246-mile mark and stood 1 011 feet (308 m) above sea level. It opened in 1888 and closed on 1 August 1963. In the early days, a Mr Cooper claimed that Outalpa meant "waterhole in a gap", while the railway place names book says it was named after "a native word, referring to water; given by Messrs Herde and Foote to their station in 1858."

Freight train working time between Wawirra and Outalpa was 19 minutes on the down and 23 minutes on the up, with running either way being reasonably easy. The first level crossing on the section lay immediately past the Wawirra siding, serving the access road into the Wawirra sheep station. Back in the days before rail, that road was the original track from Terowie to Mannahill and Silverton. After rounding a curve beyond Wawirra, the line crossed the large Wawirra Creek bridge, whose waters flowed near Outalpa and into Olary Creek. One engineman, Catta

16. Wawirra – Outalpa

*Outalpa railway station on the Cockburn line, c. 1930s.
Dort motor inspection car in the foreground.
Photo: Lionel Noble Collection.*

Outalpa railway station and signal cabin, c. 1950s. Photo: Lionel Noble.

The Cockburn Line

Miller, used to say that from there the line went 'past Radium Hill right across the border to Loch Lilly Station and spread out down there.'

On a down movement from Wawirra, there was a gradual climb to what we called the sand cutting, a spot where sand covering the line was a constant problem. They even planted seed in the cutting in 1928 to help with the issue, though it didn't work out. A telephone was installed at the 244-mile 40-chain mark so the ganger could warn the Outalpa signalman if the sand had blocked the cutting. Horse teams used to scoop out the sand were kept in temporary yards opposite the facing switches at the Mannahill end of the yard. Each day, those teams would walk along the left side of the line up to the cutting and back, about 2 miles each way. The same fellow who owned the teams, Tom Sheedy from Nackara, also worked at other spots along the Cockburn Line cleaning out railway reservoirs.

Clearing the Cockburn line at the sand cutting near Outalpa after a sand storm, c. 1950s. L: Stan Andrews, Jack White, _?. Photo: Lionel Noble Collection.

16. Wawirra – Outalpa

Engineman Ken Sleep once told me his memories of clearing the cutting:

> [T]here were about 50 men there. The Department took on all casual hands as well as the navvies. You could shift in a half day with a bulldozer more than what you could shift in a fortnight with the men. We were up on the top cutting out of Outalpa. We would take the sand down and place it on both sides of the bridges to strengthen the bank; it would be back the next day with a good east wind blowing.

In the late 1940s, my wife Lorace and I were travelling home on the Broken Hill express after a holiday in Sydney. It had been blowing a gale and it was freezing cold. Around midnight we felt a bump and the train suddenly stopped. Arthur Fuller, who was either the guard or the sleeping car conductor, hurried along the carriages asking if anyone was hurt. Apparently, the wind had been so fierce that it blew an empty cattle or sheep van about 6 miles (9.7 km) from the Mannahill yard. The mystery back then was why the vehicle hadn't derailed as its two axles passed over the derailer designed to protect the main line. Fortunately, the front of the locomotive wasn't damaged. I remember fireman Jack Asher saying that when he spotted the van in the headlight, he warned his mate, who managed to apply the emergency brake, lessening the impact. The locomotive carried on to Peterborough.

The Broken Hill express was the only train equipped with an emergency phone as part of the brake van equipment. To use it, two rods were screwed together to form a pole, with one end fitted with a T-piece. That T-piece was swung over the pair of

The Cockburn Line

telephone wires running alongside the track, one for the party line and the other for train control. It was scraped along the wires to ensure good contact, and the leads from the overhead wire were attached to the terminals of a portable boxed telephone. Then the operator turned the handle to ring the relevant code. The handset even had a switch so that when pressed, you could talk directly with train control.

Running along the flat and approaching the 244-mile sand cutting, just to the right of the line, lay the Outalpa mine diggings. I remember engineman Archie Williams telling me that Tom Reece, the owner of the Capitol Theatre in Peterborough, had once worked those very mines. He told me to see for myself the gold nuggets dangling from Tom's watch chain, said to be from the Outalpa diggings. Sure enough, the little lumps of gold were there.

Mark Noble at the Outalpa Mine near the main standard-gauge line, 1987. Photo: Lionel Noble.

The second level crossing was just past the sand cutting and required extra care because of the heavy Broken Hill main road traffic. Originally, the road ran along the right side of the line, but as the area was prone to flooding many small road bridges were needed. The bridges often ended up under water and were the scene of motor vehicle accidents. A new road was eventually built to the left of the line.

16. Wawirra – Outalpa

A small culvert under the line before entering the Outalpa yard would often flood, causing train delays. Even the smallest downpour could send water up to the bridge timbers. Although the bridge was transferred to the new formation when the standard-gauge line opened, it still became the site of the first washaway on the new line. Further changes were later made to overcome that problem.

Senior enginemen used to tell me stories about guard Bill Fenwick, who in his early days on the job was signalman at Outalpa. When rabbits were plentiful, Bill would head out to nearby properties and rig up wire netting around a dam, sometimes trapping as many as 4,000 pairs in one night. Supposedly that was how he made enough money to buy the houses he eventually owned in Peterborough. Bill, a tall, quiet, likeable fellow, was an express guard in my day. The old timers called him "Whistling Bill" because he was always softly whistling. He joined in the big poker schools in the barracks at Cockburn,

Railway gangers at Outalpa sitting on hand operated trikes, c. 1950s. Railway employee cottages are to the rear. L to R: Jock Inglis (later engineman), Lionel Summerton, Les Cook (later signalman and train controller) and Cliff Lafestry. Photo: Lionel Noble Collection.

The Cockburn Line

though he'd give himself away by starting to whistle whenever he had a good hand. The others would then toss in their cards, effectively making Bill's hand worth nothing.

On one occasion, Max Twigden was firing for engineman Bill "Brumby" Jordan. It was nearly dark when they arrived at Outalpa, and Max walked back to the humpy to fetch the electric staff for Olary. Bill decided to play a joke on him by placing a large rubber toy snake near a lighted step on the locomotive. When Max spotted it on his return, he shot up into the cabin, grabbed the big fire pricker and belted the daylights out of that imitation snake. The way the thing bounced about made him smell a rat, and before long Max was laughing his head off. That story went around the depots for quite a while.

Crossing movement at Outalpa, looking towards Mannahill, c. 1950s. The original old cottages were on the right by the trees. Photo: Lionel Noble Collection.

At the same spot, I once saw a swaggie walking along the road. He came over for a billy of hot water, but with only a 4- to 6-minute stop for a staff change, there wasn't much time for a chat. It must have been a long walk for those men of the road who didn't "jump the rattler". Old timers on the Cockburn Line recalled that rattlers were the improvised hopper trucks used to

16. Wawirra – Outalpa

convey coke to the smelters operating at the big Broken Hill Proprietary mine. These trucks were ordinary vehicles converted to hoppers by fitting them with a light framework designed to carry corrugated iron sheets fastened with bolts. After a while, the bolts would loosen, causing the iron to rattle and produce noises a bit like a tin kettle band. On the return from Broken Hill, the hoppers were either empty or loaded with heavy lead ingots, only a few of which were needed to make a full truckload. That, they said, made the vehicle suitable for the swaggie fraternity.

PM Daley once told the story of the 18-week 1892 Broken Hill strike. There was no work on the Hill, and people were leaving the city by any means as quickly as they could. In south Broken Hill, three- and four-roomed wood and iron houses were selling for whatever the owners could get, £5 or £10, any money to pay he fares. Men started to jump the rattler, and hundreds left that way. The police always combed through the goods trains before they left a railway town, so many men would walk as far as Silverton or Limestone Siding, where they were seldom spotted.

Narrow gauge freight 830 Class locomotive 867 hauling empty ore wagons at the 247-mile Outalpa, 1967. Photo: Lionel Noble.

The Cockburn Line

The Olary railway station building, 1950. Stationmaster, Michael Brown. Photo: Michael Brown.

Plummer Villa in Olary, 1964. The building was named after Jim Plummer, the standard-gauge line plate laying foreman. It was used as a barracks during standardisation. Photo: Lionel Noble.

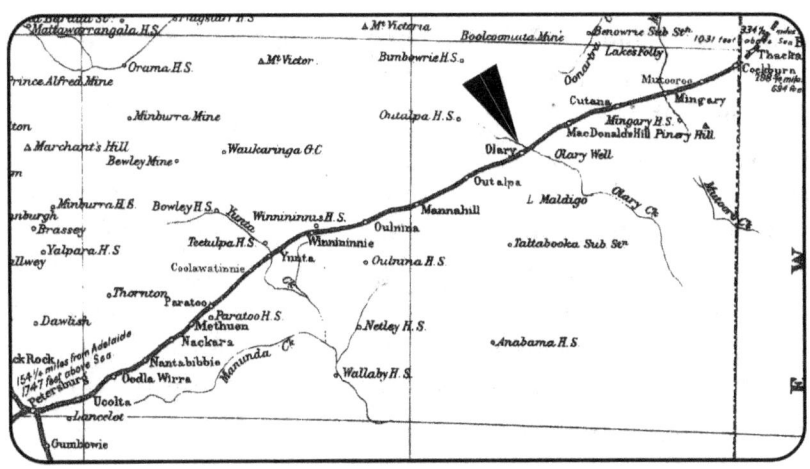

17. Outalpa – Olary

Olary was 10½ miles (16.9 km) from Outalpa and 102¾ miles (165.4 km) from Peterborough

Olary station siding was at the 257-mile mark and stood at 929 feet (283 m) above sea level. It opened on 14 June 1887 and closed on 30 June 1963. The name Olary was thought to be a corruption of the native name "Oolarie", though its meaning is not recorded. The SAR book of station names says, "It was first given, about 1870, to a well by Messrs Duffield, Harrold and Hurd, who held the country under a pastoral lease." The scheduled running time for the section was 27 minutes on the down and 30 minutes on the up. It had only one level crossing— where the old Broken Hill main road to the south, passed over the line to the north at the 250-mile 20-chain point.

In my day, all the railway cottages at Olary were on the station side of the yard, that is, the southern side. Three maintenance cottages were on the main street (the northern side) at the Cutana end of the yard, along with the stationmaster's and signalman's houses. During standardisation, the signalman's house was

The Cockburn Line

known as "Plummer Villa", named for Jim Plummer, the plate laying foreman of the line construction gang.

Immediately after leaving the Outalpa yard, there was a short down grade of 1-in-120. When coming from Olary and having to stop at Outalpa to take the passing siding, many trains had trouble restarting. You could always hear the rumble as a locomotive went over the damaged rail caused by previous engines trying to lift the load into the yard. It was one of the tight spots on the Cockburn Line; apart from that section, the line undulated gently with slight up and down grades where speed was easily maintained.

Washaway at the 248/249 mile, Outalpa - Olary section, 28 November 1933. Photo: Lionel Noble Collection.

Special care had to be taken between Outalpa and Olary during thunderstorms. A lack of bridges often caused severe embankment and track damage, and the bridges that did exist were frequently blocked with trees and other debris. In 1933, 1946, 1947 and 1950, the Cockburn Line experienced heavy flooding, with the Outalpa to Olary section hit worst of all. In

17. Outalpa – Olary

Washaway at the 248/249 mile, Outalpa – Olary section, 28 November 1933. Photo: Lionel Noble Collection.

1933, nearly a mile of line was washed away between the 247- and 249-mile marks. Engineman Ken Sleep recalled seeing water rising to the line ballast, and the old enginemen said it was the most severe flood damage along the Cockburn Line. On the north side, the water rose to the top of the embankment until it finally gave way. Such was the force and volume of water that the washed-away line was rolled over like a piece of hoop iron. Evidence of the flood remained for years.

Around that area, the first major standard-gauge derailment occurred due to a buckle in the track. The derailed train was the first "jet" to run from Peterborough to Broken Hill on 24 January 1970 and was crewed by engineman Bob Hams, Acting Loco Inspector Max Twigden and fireman Eric Rann. Twenty-three wagons derailed initially. After a delay, the front part of the train was sent to Cutana. However, after crossing Olary Creek, an additional five wagons carrying new motor vehicles also derailed, leaving only the locomotives and crew to continue to Cutana.

The Cockburn Line

The first derailment on the standard-gauge line, 1970 at the 268 mile between Olary and Outalpa. Photo: Lionel Noble.

Harry Lively carted sand from Olary Creek, which was then loaded onto trucks on the main freight loop at Olary. The trucks took the sand to narrow-gauge depots where it was dried and sorted for use in locomotive sand boxes. At the depot, workers shovelled the sand by hand into a rotating, perforated drum that removed stones as the sand fell into a hopper. While the drum turned, an oil-burning flame dried the sand. Finally, the sorted sand was transferred into trucks or drums based on what was needed, and thousands of tons were used each year throughout the Division.

Stan Andrews was a riding ganger stationed at Mannahill with Frank O'Riley, who later became the district foreman's clerk. The riding ganger's main duty was spotting issues along the line: degraded sleepers, loose dog spikes, switches, fish plates, crossing and bridge timbers, track defects and damaged fences. Each morning when signing on duty, the gangers would confer with the district foreman by party line to be allocated their tasks for the day, and then the riding ganger returned the next day to check on the work.

17. Outalpa – Olary

Olary railway gangers, 1950. L to R: Stan Andrews (District Foreman), T Davidson, V Hocking, B Brant, R Dunk. Photo: Lionel Noble.

Olary railway gangers, 1945. L to R: Ivan Haddrill, Joe Woodall, Howard Casey, Peter Moroney, Ozcar Zilm, Tom Davidson. Photo: Lionel Noble Collection.

Railway porter and former Olary ganger Peter Moroney at the Peterborough railway station, 1967. Photo: Lionel Noble.

The Cockburn Line

Olary's surface water was good for locomotives, but bore water was a different matter as it left scale on the boiler's interior and caused the locomotive to prime. A water treatment program on the Cockburn Line began in the 1950s, when ALFLOC powder was added to hard water and SBMS powder to surface water. Each time water was added to the tender, a measured volume of powder was included. Eventually, water for the locomotives and the town at Olary was drawn from three reservoirs, two on the north and one on the south side of town.

Alfloc instruction notice, usually attached to a water column for filling steam trains. Alfloc was an additive used to condition the poor quality water. Photo: Lionel Noble.

I remember two accidents in the Olary yard. In one, a train standing on the down main was smashed into at the rear, doing extensive damage to an attached passenger car and brake van. The other took place at the Cutana end when a movement entered the yard against a stop signal. I never learned the full details of either accident.

On one occasion in 1953, I arrived at Olary on a 300-class locomotive and stopped on the up main line to take water at the Outalpa end of the yard. As my mate filled the tanks with water, I examined and oiled the locomotive. While checking, I discovered that the right-hand leading connecting rod was bent, a repair that required pulling down the side on that unit. I set about uncoupling the rods. The job was going well until, while

17. Outalpa – Olary

pushing a pin out with my finger and holding the combination lever with my other hand, the tapered, greasy lever slipped through my hand, jamming my right finger in the valve spindle's combination lever pin hole. Fortunately, my fireman heard me calling and freed my finger, though its top was badly cut and had swollen to the size of a banana. We walked from the Outalpa end of the yard to the station where I nearly passed out from the pain. Someone gave me a sip of brandy while guard Trixie Munro and stationmaster G Richardson bandaged my finger. Trixie's hand was shaking so badly it didn't help matters at all. He'd had a night out at Cockburn, and I wasn't sure who was suffering more. After another engineman relieved me, I then travelled back to Peterborough in the brake van on my own train until I was picked up at Paratoo by an MIC (motor inspection car).

300-class locomotive 300.
Fireman John Borbas and engineman C Mann.
Photo: Lionel Noble Collection.

When I arrived at Peterborough, I walked over Railway Terrace to see Dr. Stan Martin who was playing tennis. He told me to go to the hospital so he could attend to me. The accident

The Cockburn Line

had happened at 8.00 am, but it wasn't until 4.30 pm that I was finally seen at the hospital. There were no taxis or car relief back then. Trixie and the stationmaster had wrapped my finger well, and the congealed blood on the bandage had sealed the wound. The bleeding had stopped, but it was a severe cut that needed stitches. With my arm in a sling after treatment, I walked to my house across from the hospital. As I made my way down the driveway, my 3-year-old daughter Meryn spotted me with my bandaged hand and ran into the house in tears. It was quite some time before she'd have anything to do with me.

On another occasion, I was firing to Cockburn with engineman Arthur Bain. We were on the tucker train, and by the time we reached Olary, shunting en route, the train length had shortened. Normally, when a freight train arrived in a station yard, the guard and the local traffic employee would confer about the work to be done. I could hear the traffic employee shouting something, clearly trying to get my attention because he wanted us to perform a shunt before the opposing train arrived. Seeing a bit of smoke off in the distance, I could tell the train was still several miles away, so I suggested to Arthur that I'd go over to the shop and get a cool drink.

Gonga told him, 'You'd better not go on like that with him; he's the best fighter in Peterborough.'

On my way back to the locomotive, I stopped by the stationmaster's office to ask when the other train was expected and to find out what all the commotion was about. I walked into the humpy and asked the porter, 'What were you singing out about out there?'

He immediately became apologetic and excited. 'It's all right,' he said, 'we all get uptight at times.'

I didn't quite understand what he was on about until sometime later when our guard, Gordon "Gonga" Wight, explained on our arrival at McDonald's Hill. The porter had been

17. Outalpa – Olary

abusing me because I hadn't been watching for his instructions on arriving at Olary. Gonga told him, 'You'd better not go on like that with him; he's the best fighter in Peterborough.' When I'd walked into the office and said what I did, the porter thought I might be after him. Gonga and I laughed about that for years.

Peterborough railway guard Gordon 'Gonga' Wight with 50½ years of service, 1969. Note Gordon's locally made tucker box, a very familiar sight in Peterborough in the railway days. Photo: Lionel Noble.

Once, while coming home from Cockburn, a chap walked up to us at Olary and asked if he could get a ride on the engine. I told him to ask the driver since I was only the fireman. My mate Tim Jenkins agreed to let him on. We talked for several miles, and he turned out to be an interesting fellow. He was a returned WWII soldier who'd been in Changi camp, where he'd had a very rough time as a prisoner. The man loved trains and figured that

The Cockburn Line

travelling around the state would help him recover from the horrors of Changi. As it turned out, he was an engineer who'd earlier worked in a tin mine up in the islands, and he asked if he could have a try at firing the engine. Tim agreed, and he did very well as it was clear it wasn't the first time he'd swung a shovel.

After we arrived home, I was in the YMCA lounge where I was boarding when I got a phone call to go down to the Railway Hotel and see a Mr. So-and-So (I can't recall his name). He showed me some excellent watercolour drawings of steam engines that he'd done while in Changi. Looking back later, I realised he must have been a brilliant but modest man. I wished I could have caught up with him again, but I never saw him once more.

Olary railway station, 1987. Photo: Lionel Noble.

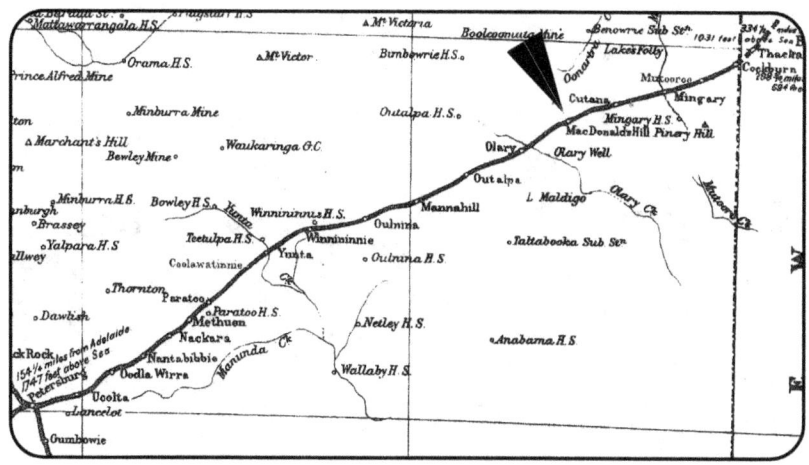

18. Olary – McDonald's Hill

McDonald's Hill was 9 miles (14.5 km) from Olary and 111¾ miles (179.8 km) from Peterborough

McDonald's Hill was named by Surveyor Brooks after one of his men and stood 879 feet (268 m) above sea level. The station opened for traffic on 14 June 1887 and closed on 30 June 1963. Only a passing siding and the main line were in the yard. The station yard wasn't level as it ran slightly uphill toward the Cutana end; all the buildings were on the north side of the line. The humpy that housed the electric staff instruments and telephones was larger than most along the Cockburn Line, flanked by two or three large trees and the gangers' quarters which was a sturdy stone building.

Four level crossings were on the section. The first was immediately upon leaving Olary, while the others allowed vehicle access from the Broken Hill road to a large property south of the line. The last crossing near McDonald's Hill, toward the end of the down grade, was removed during my time.

The Cockburn Line

McDonald's Hill railway station and employee cottages, c. 1970s.
Photo: Alex Grunbach. Used with permission of the
Australian Railway Historical Society, NSW.

Departing over the first level crossing at Olary and running to McDonald's Hill was a reasonably easy run. Gum Creek (or Olary Creek as it was also called) lay a little over a mile from Olary, and heavier steaming was needed up to the 261-mile 60-chain curve, followed by a run of three-quarters of a mile and then light steaming up to the top cutting at the 264-mile mark. From there, it was a down grade to McDonald's Hill station yard. On the up, a 1 in 120 grade had to be negotiated for about two miles to the top cutting. From that point to the 262-mile, the train drifted, steamed again to the top of the hill at the 261-mile 60-chain, then ran down to the Olary Creek bridge and light steamed into Olary. The scheduled running time for freight trains was 25 minutes down and 30 minutes up.

It was always interesting at McDonald's Hill to watch an approaching train from Cutana as its smoke could be seen from a long distance. On windless days, the smoke bellowed straight up from the locomotive and it was quite a sight as the engine rounded the curve. Senior enginemen used to say that if the smoke left the funnel and rolled over the boiler straight to the ground, it was a sign of rain or a change in the weather. I found that to be true.

Climbing out of the McDonald's Hill yard on an up movement was often tricky as it required heavy steaming. Standing on the passing siding, you could almost read the minds of the ap-

18. Olary – McDonald's Hill

proaching train crews; they were all looking for that green flag from the guard in the middle of the yard that gave their train permission to run straight through. Running through rather than starting from scratch was a huge advantage, especially for stock trains, which were always the heaviest. If it rained or there was a strong side wind, the locomotive's wheels would easily slip. The problem was made worse when, upon arriving at McDonald's Hill, there was very little steam or even enough boiler water to have a shave!

After stopping at the facing switches on an up movement, many enginemen found it necessary to let the train run back a short distance and then try again to lift the load into the Cutana end of the yard. Where possible, the up train was given the main line. An engineman on a down movement approaching the yard would do his best to let the up train enter first. If time permitted, the down train guard would book in and obtain an electric staff for the up movement, enabling the train to run straight through. It always took a combined effort by the crews.

> **Senior enginemen used to say that if the smoke left the funnel and rolled over the boiler straight to the ground, it was a sign of rain or a change in the weather. I found that to be true.**

Tom Fitzgerald told the story of "Jock the Fireman" (or "Egotistical Jock" as he was known, his swaggering gait hinting at a fine opinion of himself). Tom wrote:

> *A run through McDonald's Hill used to be considered helpful in getting over the stiff grade ahead. With the object of impressing the crew of a waiting train, Jock contrived to approach with the white feather flying and a cloud of black smoke soaring skywards from the funnel.*[19]

[19.] The "white feather" or "feather flying" phenomenon occurred when a locomotive ran at full boiler pressure, causing its safety valves to emit a fine wisp of steam.

The Cockburn Line

Then, leaning out of the cab with one leg dangling from his seat, his cap pulled over one ear and pipe in his mouth, he would go sailing through the yard with an air of assumed indifference too obvious to deceive.

One hot Sunday in the Cockburn barracks a pair of wags, badly in need of a reviver, conceived the idea of playing on Jock's vanity. Noticing him cooling off under the veranda they started a conversation intended for his ears. 'Yes,' said one, 'there can be no doubt that Jock is easily the best fireman in the Division.' The other readily agreed, adding that he would give pounds to be able to run through McDonald's Hill with the feather flying. The expected soon happened. Sauntering around the corner, as if unaware of their presence, Jock spoke of the heat and suggested a walk to the Border Gate Hotel. No pressing was needed, and forever after he became as good as ready money to the two kidders.

An early flying gang, c. 1900s. While this particular gang was based on the Great Northern Rail Line, the gangs of the Cockburn Line would have been similar. Photo: Mrs O'Connell.

18. Olary – McDonald's Hill

McDonald's Hill was one of the main spots where the flying gang camped using one of the old station buildings. Back then, the gangs along the line were well staffed with four or five men in each gang, usually stationed at every main siding. There weren't any mechanical wonders to lift and pack the line; it was all done by hand. The cook for the McDonald's Hill and Cutana gang was Jack Coffey, a likeable person who seemed to be there for years. Jack had a radio that could pick up not only Adelaide stations but also ones over the border. As soon as the train pulled into McDonald's Hill, he'd update the guard on news of interest such as boxing match results, horse races and the like. Every time we walked back to the humpy to change the electric staff, the crews wondered what the news of the day might be.

I remember times when the section flooded. The small culvert at the 262-mile 60-chain often had floodwaters spilling over it, washing away ballast on both sides of the line. Another area always prone to flooding was on the down grade between the third level crossing and Olary Creek. Water would run off the side of the hill, over the Broken Hill road and along the north side of the railway line until there was so much that it spread over the track, taking the ballast with it. This situation was finally rectified when the standard-gauge line was built.

It was at McDonald's Hill that I had to carry out one of my most awkward repair jobs which was on a 300-class Garratt locomotive. When the 300-class first arrived on the Division, they were driven tender first which meant the boiler section was at the rear. They also arrived without enclosed sides, so in winter it was unbearably cold for the engineman and fireman. Being oil burners, the 300-class not only meant there was no shovelling but also no heat entering the cabin through an open firebox door. If the fireman dared open the door, the glare was so bright it interfered with the engineman's vision. It was simply a matter of grinning and bearing it. Eventually, side doors were fitted, and that made a huge difference. Imagine standing on a platform in the open, in the middle of winter, travelling at 20–30 mph (32–

The Cockburn Line

300-class locomotive on the Cockburn line with the short end leading, c. 1950s. Photo: Lionel Noble Collection.

48 kph) with the firebox right behind you! I even purchased an old army coat from an Adelaide disposal store to keep warm. When turning facilities were later introduced at Cockburn, the Garratt started leading funnel first.

We had arrived at McDonald's Hill at night and were on the line closest to the humpy waiting to cross an oncoming train. I could smell a hot bearing or something like it, so I took a look and found that one of the front left-hand coupled wheel axle boxes was running hot. These boxes were greased with a hard grease pack, shaped to fit the lower part of the journal and held in place by a cover and two pins. Two spare grease packs were kept in a container on the locomotive. It might sound like an easy repair job—remove the pins and cover, scrape out the old grease and slip in a new pack—but the problem was there was no pit to work in. That meant I had to climb through the locomotive frame and squeeze into a tight space just to do the replacement.

I had another incident at McDonald's Hill when I was an engineman. I'd been issued a train order at Olary to take the main line at McDonald's Hill and cross train No. 600 up, "but do not

18. Olary – McDonald's Hill

enter the yard until train 600 has arrived". We could see the opposing train's headlight in the distance and knew it was on its way, yet we had to stand at the facing switches for a long time as that light didn't seem to be getting any closer. Finally, train 600 arrived and entered the yard on the main line. It turned out that the delay had been caused by a swarm of grasshoppers near the 273-mile crossing, a short distance from Cutana. That meant the train had to be split and its leading vehicles shunted about 8 miles (12.9 km) into McDonald's Hill and placed on the siding. Jack Altman, the engineman in charge of train 600, went back to pick up the rest of his train and ended up on that section for hours. At that time the Cutana siding was closed, so the section between Mingary and McDonald's Hill stretched about 22 miles. When the whole train consist was finally re-coupled, we pulled into the main line. Their guard, Vincent Govette, handed me the electric staff and explained what had happened and how long they'd been delayed. Then we set off for Mingary.

> **Apparently, having two electric staffs wasn't a rule violation as long as one of them was the appropriate staff for that section.**

As we ran through the Cutana yard, I recall checking the time, an all-important chore for the driver, and noticed that we had two electric staffs, one on the brake valve and the other on the lubricator. When we arrived at Mingary, I spoke with the train controller, Joe Murphy. 'Are you collecting metal?' he asked. He pointed that out because I had two staffs in my possession. Train No. 600 was still at McDonald's Hill and running very low on tender water, while train No. 531, the important produce train for Broken Hill, was delayed at Olary. I couldn't sleep at Cockburn that night, thinking about how I'd love to be firing again! Eventually, I was asked to submit a report and never heard any more about it. Apparently, having two electric staffs wasn't a rule violation as long as one of them was the appropriate staff for that section. Vincent may have had some explaining to do!

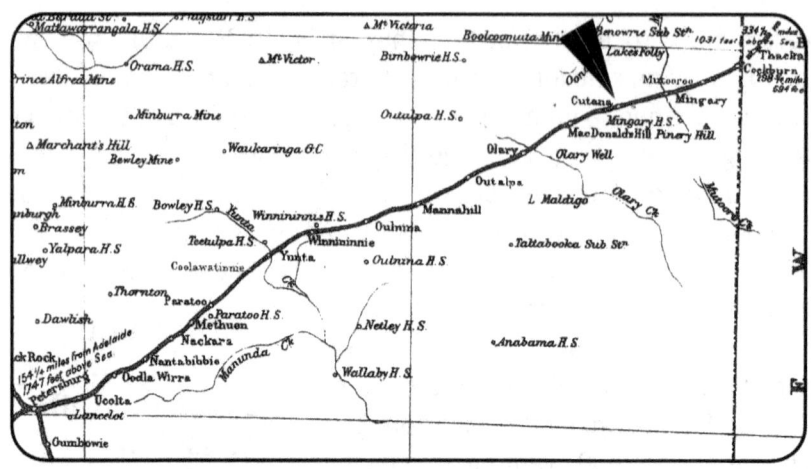

19. McDonald's Hill – Cutana

Cutana was 9 miles (14.5 km) from McDonald's Hill and 120¾ miles (194.3 km) from Peterborough

Cutana station, located at the 274¾-mile marker, opened in 1888 and stood 683 feet (208.2 m) above sea level. The name means "waterhole on plain", but a museum record suggests it may mean "woman's digging stick, place". The railway yard itself wasn't level but sloped toward the Mingary end. In later years there was just one level crossing on the section, at about the 272-mile marker. There were two main creeks, Acocia Creek and Lux Creek.

In the original railway yard, three railway cottages faced Cutana on the south side of the nearby Cartwright pastoral station. There were mail stables and a hut on the road side that provided facilities for travellers on the track to and from Terowie. It was usually a good spot to see kangaroos returning from the Cartwright Station dams.

On down working, a train would practically run on its own out of the McDonald's Hill yard. After departure, and once

19. McDonald's Hill – Cutana

*Cutana railway station, yard and employee cottages c. 1960s.
To the right is the spur line to Radium Hill, along with ballast mounds.
Main line in the centre and passing siding to the left. Photo: Lionel Noble.*

*600-class locomotive 600 at the Radium Hill ballast bin, 1965.
Photo: Lionel Noble.*

The Cockburn Line

around the curve to the right, the train ran for several miles, steamed again for a short distance, then ran nearly to Cutana where the load was "picked up".[20] At that point, light steaming was necessary to reach the yard limit board, from where the train drifted into the yard.

Cutana was a place that frequently flooded, causing problems not only for the railway but also for motorists. I remember occasions near Cutana along the Broken Hill road on my way to the Hill when I couldn't see any road for miles because of the water. The only way to follow the road was by watching the guideposts, which were few and far between before the road was sealed. Flooding often occurred in the Cutana yard, mainly at the McDonald's Hill end.

From Cutana, an 11-mile (17.7 km) spur line was constructed to serve the Radium Hill mine, allowing concentrates to be railed to either Port Pirie or Adelaide. Construction began in April 1953, and the line officially opened on 2 November that year, with the first mixed train operating the following day. Initially built as narrow gauge, the line was converted to standard gauge in the mid-1960s. During this transition, the original sleepers were re-bored, and every fourth sleeper was replaced with a new one suited for standard-gauge rails. Mixed trains took approximately 32 minutes to reach Radium Hill, with the return journey taking around 42 minutes. Passenger services also operated to and from Adelaide. T-class locomotives were used on the narrow-gauge line, and locomotive T-232 was a regular on the route between Peterborough and Radium Hill. It was equipped with a Flaman-type speed recorder, akin to those found on the more powerful broad-gauge engines.

At one time there were large gangs in tents along the railway fence on the main road side. They were a wild lot. One Saturday, while working home to Peterborough, I went back to the humpy

---

[20.] Enginemen used this term when it was necessary to take up the slack in the train's load. This action helped the locomotive negotiate slight grades or resume steaming after drifting.

19. McDonald's Hill – Cutana

with guard Roy Hogg to change the electric staff. While we were both in the cabin, a large chap from one of the gangs stood in the doorway, almost filling it. For some reason, he was in an aggressive mood, with fists clenched and ready to reshape every human being on earth. He was inviting Roy and me to shape up or get murdered, claiming he'd shot better men in the war than us. It was every man for himself, and I edged myself behind the electric staff instruments while quietly working out my moves. Then Roy, a returned soldier, mentioned something about the 27th Regiment, and that did wonders. I grabbed the electric staff and took off, leaving the two buddies to talk about the war. I got on the locomotive, pulled the train ahead and Roy shot out of the humpy and jumped on the brake van step as it passed. The battle was won.

I was firing for George Miller on a weekend Broken Hill express to Cockburn. Catta often took his bicycle with him on a weekend trip so he could ride out looking for kangaroos to shoot or take a training ride over the 30 miles (48.3 km) from Cockburn to Broken Hill. George was a quiet sort who always had to be on the move, and he never stayed around the barracks. On that trip he had his rifle with him in the cabin and, as we left McDonald's Hill around dawn, he told me to call out if I spotted a roo. He sat on his seat with the rifle between his legs and the barrel pointing upward. Near the Cartwright dams I yelled out to let George know I'd spotted a roo on my side. Unfortunately, George had forgotten his earlier request and was startled by my calling. He jumped, the gun went off, and it blew a hole in the cabin roof, leaving George with an awful look on his face.

Alan Welsby, the last qualified locomotive instructor stationed on the Peterborough Division, was working on the up ore train on 23 April 1961 when he suffered a serious accident between McDonald's Hill and Cutana. Alan recalled the details:

The Cockburn Line

It was assumed that someone had shot holes in the dam float at Mingary, causing the down pipe to drop in the mud. Mud and water were then pumped into the overhead tank. I didn't realise that so much mud was in the water, having had no previous experience with that sort of thing. The mud wiped out the lead safety plugs on the locomotive, the tube plate went and the firebox door blew open. I was sprayed with boiling mud.

My fireman, Neville Madex, and I walked back to the brake van for first aid. I didn't realise I had been badly burnt, so when we were nearly to the van shock took over and my body shook uncontrollably. Fortunately, the Cockburn loco foreman was driving past in his car as the incident happened and he took me to the Radium Hill Hospital where I remained until I was stable enough to travel by car to Peterborough. I stayed in the Peterborough hospital for a week and was then taken by ambulance to Wakefield Street Hospital in Adelaide for a further week. It was thought I would require skin grafts on the backs of both hands, but it was eventually found to be unnecessary. I was off work for 13 weeks, and the locomotive was also out of commission for about the same length of time.

Peterborough loco inspector Alan Welsby, 1969. Photo: Lionel Noble.

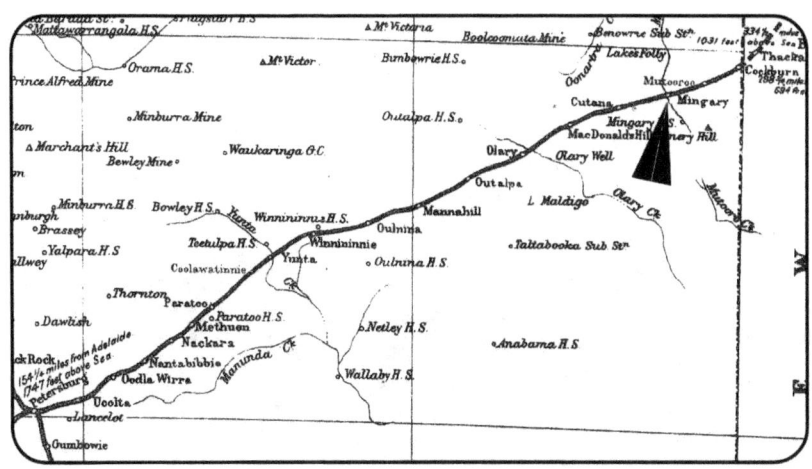

20. Cutana – Mingary

Mingary was 8¼ miles (13.3 km) from Cutana and 129 miles (207.6 km) from Peterborough

Mingary station stood at 603 feet (183.8 m) above sea level and opened on 14 June 1887. The town was surrounded by saltbush which was excellent feed for the thousands of sheep which roamed the vast nearby properties. Mingary was the lowest station along the Cockburn Line; over the 100 miles (161 km) between Nantabibbie and Mingary, the line dropped 1 208 feet (368.2 m).

Some confusion remains about the derivation and meaning of the name "Mingary". According to Mr Cooper, an early surveyor, it meant "place for wattle". Geoffrey Manning's book, however, describes it as "a town near Cockburn, proclaimed on 15 September 1892", and states that it's an Aboriginal word meaning "the northern-most waterhole". Then, *SAR Stations, With Their Meanings and Derivations* simply states it's a native name whose meaning is unknown.

The section of track to Mingary was easy for the crew, thanks to its gentle undulations. Train speed could be kept constant

The Cockburn Line

The original Mingary station buildings with the power plant building to the far right, c. 1950s. Photo: Lionel Noble Collection.

with little alteration to the regulator or valve and the trip from Cutana took about 24 minutes. Running into Mingary yard was more like drifting. On an up movement from Mingary, the locomotive steamed heavily; after reaching the second crossing that pressure was eased. Even though things were steady from there to Cutana, a full head of steam was needed all the way.

The first of the four level crossings on this stretch was about 1 to 2 miles (1.61 to 3.2 km) from the Cutana yard. It was originally the main Broken Hill road crossing until it was moved toward Mingary when the new bitumen road to Broken Hill was built. On that crossing, on 27 June 1968, Mannahill district foreman Frank Buick lost his life in a collision with a motor vehicle while driving a ganger's quad in broad daylight.

Travelling toward Mingary and its large creek, the second level crossing gave access to Bulloo Creek Station, Boolcoomatta homestead and other properties on the north side of Mingary Creek. The third crossing was at the top of a slight grade, and the final one was right at the Cutana end of the Mingary yard and was

20. Cutana – Mingary

used by traffic heading behind the station. One nearby bridge was close to a cluster of railway cottages and a small reservoir built in the early days, just inside the railway fence on the south side.

Located at the 278-mile, the old Koolka siding once served a flux mine seven miles to the south, the ore of which was used in Broken Hill mine operations. It was possible to still see the old track formation which had cut a path through the trees as it crossed the main Broken Hill road on the south side of the line. Pieces of red ore littered the ground where the old formation joined the main line. The siding had been opened on 27 July 1893 and was removed in 1898, and standardisation removed all remaining evidence of the line having been there.

The track in this section was built to a lesser standard than the rest of the line, presumably as a cost- and time-saving measure.

The type of line construction for this section was quite different from the old standard. It was basically a surface

Railway employees at Mingary, c. 1940s. L to R: Dave Bradshaw, _?, _?, Ross Robb. Photo: Lionel Noble Collection.

The Cockburn Line

*Mingary railway yard with the railway employee cottages to the top, 1948.
Photo: Lionel Noble Collection.*

*300-class locomotive 305 stands on the passing siding at Mingary, 1953.
The signalman, hand in pocket for his keys, walks up to the Mutooroo
end of the yard to set the switches, while engineman Lionel Noble looks on.
Photo: Lionel Noble Collection.*

20. Cutana – Mingary

line that avoided heavy earthworks by taking advantage of frequent grade changes, only bridging creeks when absolutely necessary. Wherever possible, creeks or low depressions were crossed at surface level. The track designers expected floods to be rare due to the limited rainfall. They also assumed that, even if a flood did occur, it would only cause a brief delay in traffic. They also reduced the amount of ballast under the sleepers to keep the structure lightweight. The anticipated speeds were a leisurely 15 mph (24 kph) for passenger trains and 12 mph (19.3 kph) for goods and mixed trains.[21]

The irony in that "limited rainfall" remark can't be overlooked. Sure, rainfall was limited, but hardly anyone could predict when thunderstorms would roll in. And roll in they did, with storms doing all the damage. A small culvert about three quarters of a mile from the original Cutana formation became the site of a 1928 derailment. Floodwaters washed out the culvert, and T-class locomotive 245 overturned, killing fireman Phil Middleton. Peterborough engineman Jim Ritchie, who was driving a shunting locomotive at Cockburn at the time, was sent with his mate to help clear up the derailment.

Engineman Paddy Harding recalled the incident this way:

Phil Middleton was killed, engine 245, Jack Bond driver, Wally Kaehne guard (retired years ago as a yardmaster); that was in 1928. I was fireman for 'Sparks' Thomas on the train ahead. We were at Nackara when we got the news. It was a flash flood; there wasn't a drop of water when we went through Cutana. You will notice on one of the photographs a hole dug under the tender, it's held up with a jack. That's where Jim Ritchie got Phil out; they

---

[21.] From a paper prepared by the SAR, "The Peterborough Division of Narrow-Gauge Lines." Further details unknown.

reckon they never seen a man work like Jim did that day. Bondy jumped out his side unhurt, but Phil, who was trying to get out his side, was jammed between the engine and tender handrails. Wally Kaehne never went back on the road again.

Since Phil Middleton was a Quorn man, the SAR ran a special rail car to take his workmates from Peterborough to his funeral at Quorn.

Peterborough engineman Joe "Paddy" Harding at the controls of the Western Endeavour historical train across Australia, 1970. Photo: M Billett.

Accident at Cutana, 1928. Fireman Middleton (from Quorn) was killed. The accident happened over a small washed out culvert a short distance from the Cutana yard on the Mingary side. Photo: Lionel Noble Collection.

20. Cutana – Mingary

Accident at Cutana in which fireman Middleton was killed, 1928. The tender was jacked up by Jim Ritchie to dig out Phil Middleton. Photo: Lionel Noble Collection.

Members of the railway bridge gang on the Cockburn line, 1934. Rear: Joe 'Paddy' Harding; L to R: Stan Marsland, Jack Freer, Joe Dueter and Snowy ? Photo: Lionel Noble Collection.

The Cockburn Line

600-class standard-gauge work train at the 278 mile between Cutana and Mingary, c. 1970. The chimney on the tree (centre) was placed there in 1934 by Peterborough engineman Paddy Harding. Photo: Lionel Noble.

A temporary camp was set up at that same spot in the 1930s for the men working on the bridges, including Peterborough engineman Paddy Harding. It was during the Depression and there wasn't enough work in Peterborough for all the men to be regularly employed. Paddy recalled being let off the tucker train late one afternoon and having to set up camp right in the middle of a thunderstorm. 'Two inches (50.8 mm) of rain poured down, flooding the creek. There was nowhere to go, no people, no train, no motor vehicles, no protection... nothing at all.' Around 1970, Paddy pointed out the spot where, back in 1934 during his time at the gangers' camp, he had placed the top of a copper chimney in a tree to mark the location.

Mingary was always a busy siding. There was once a general store where I bought tinned Leeton's NSW cut apricots and other goods you couldn't get in SA. A small home, right next to the hall on the south side of the main street, belonged to a Miss Maxwell. Train crews often looked over to see the bonneted little old lady standing at her front gate, her dress nearly brushing the ground and with cats everywhere. The shop owner's home was

20. Cutana – Mingary

The railway cottages at Mingary. The relief signalman's hut was also used by the electrical fitter who regularly serviced the power station in the railway yard. The oldest cottages were the last two on the right. Photo: Lionel Noble Collection.

next door on the Cutana side. The shop, post office and house were all built of galvanised iron, which must have been unbearably hot in summer. There weren't any air conditioners back then, and electric power in town was switched on only on Monday mornings for washing and in the evenings for lighting.

Just south of the rail yard and across the Broken Hill road toward the railway reservoir stood the early Mingary eating-house and galvanised iron stables. The stables were used by coach company Hill and Co. for changing horses, and the eating-house fed travellers and teamsters en route to Silverton and Broken Hill. A couple of railway houses (much like those at Outalpa, Olary and Peterborough West) and a private house stood at the Cutana end of the railway yard. These were for the stationmaster, signalman and pumper. One of the cottages housed a ganger's family of 12 children. One day I was taking water from the column directly opposite the house and noticed kids all over the place. I remarked to my mate, Cliff Sleep, wondering how they could possibly sleep so many children in such a small space. 'Easy,' Cliff said. 'Just put the first lot to bed and, once they're asleep, haul 'em out and line 'em up in the corner, then put the next lot in!'

The Cockburn Line

I remember that ganger well. Every time he and his gang were out working on the line, he never failed to wave a yellow flag to warn the train to take it easy in that area. He never missed a beat, though I'd say he might have done well to have waved the flag in his bedroom!

The railway reservoirs were regularly cleaned by horse teams using scoops. Sometimes even camel teams were used in the earlier days. And when there was no water at Mingary, the supply was taken from the pipeline running from Umberumberka (NSW) to Radium Hill.

98-year-old Mrs Eileen Smith from Cockburn told me about the great times they had at Mingary with the tennis club that used leased land on the Cutana end of the yard. The courts were removed in 1914.

Peterborough engineman George 'Catta' Miller, 1973. George is holding an oil can and a slush lamp. In the early days of the railway, the lamp was often the only source of light for the engineman and fireman when a breakdown occurred at night. Photo: Lionel Noble.

Former railway guard and Jamestown stationmaster Jack Kelly at Jamestown on the eve of his retirement, 1974. Photo: Lionel Noble.

20. Cutana – Mingary

I was once working from Cockburn on No. 444 up with engineman George Miller and guard Jack Kelly. We left at 3:50 pm with a short, fully loaded ore train that included a Dolly Varden brake van, and we had a train order to cross the tucker train at Mingary.[22] While we were running between Mingary and Mutooroo over the Three Mile Creek at the 287-mile 19-chain mark, the rear seven vehicles of our consist derailed. The brake van ended up on its side with Jack Kelly still inside. George and I ran back to see if Jack was hurt. We couldn't see him at first, but we soon heard him yelling abuse. He climbed out through a door, stood on the van, then jumped to the ground, throwing his cap down and cursing about the 'bloody rotten track.' Jack was one to get off his bike very easily and that day he certainly had enough to get off his bike about! We thought he'd been hit on the head by the way he was performing.

Re-righting the Dolly Varden brake van following a derailment near Mingary, c. 1950s. Photo: Lionel Noble Collection.

[22.] A Dolly Varden brake van had a goods compartment at one end and a comfortable passenger compartment with a toilet at the other. It also featured entry steps at the passenger compartment end. In contrast, other brake vans offered seating at both ends with side doors, but boarding from ground level was more challenging.

The Cockburn Line

In cases like these, there were certain rules we had to obey: rear end protection for the train, recording the last number of the vehicle on the rails and having lights on when it got dark. We proceeded into Mingary while Jack kept watch over what was left at the derailment site using hand signals and detonators. If the last vehicle on the leading consist wasn't air-equipped, the fireman would ride the step of that vehicle into the next station in case of a breakaway. But that day everything was fully air-equipped, so I got to ride in comfort on the locomotive.

It was dusk by the time we got into the Mingary yard. The tucker train was already waiting with Paddy Harding and Norman Youngman on crew. After another delay, a Casey Jones was sent from Cockburn to the derailment site, and Paddy Harding along with the tucker train guard were taken out by the Mingary gang. George, Paddy, Jack and the other guard were then ferried back to Cockburn. The rest of our train and the locomotive were left on the freight siding. The tucker train was shunted to the dead-end line behind the station, and both locomotives were stabled (meaning the fires were knocked out and the boilers filled with water). Norman and I were practically dumped at Mingary, left to fend for ourselves since we were needed to light up the locomotives the next day.

We ended up sleeping on the kitchen floor, though that wasn't ideal with scorpions and fat centipedes lurking.

We managed to get into the empty ganger's house (the one with all the children I mentioned earlier). At least the kitchen had a fireplace where we could boil water and have a cold shower to wash off some of the day's dirt. We ended up sleeping on the kitchen floor, though that wasn't ideal with scorpions and fat centipedes lurking. Had I known they'd made their home there, I'd have chosen the bath or even the laundry sink instead. I knew there were scorpions around the water column opposite the cottage, but I never thought they'd venture indoors. Having

20. Cutana – Mingary

survived the night, we lit up the locomotives next morning and the crew arrived later by quad.

One day, leaving Cockburn and running to Mingary, the steam valve cock broke off the steam manifold. That manifold supplied steam to the burner, and when it broke, fuel oil sprayed into the firebox. I was running an oil/coal-burning locomotive, which meant that halfway to Mingary I had to switch to hand-firing with coal. With only 97 baskets of coal on the tender, it was imperative that I make repairs, and fast. I remember patching it up by blanking off the open area, breaking off a broom handle, shaping it with my pocketknife to fit, and wiring the piece of wood securely in place so the steam valve wouldn't blow out when opened. It worked out, and I reckon the delay at Mingary was no more than 15 minutes.

Peterborough locomotive inspector Jack O'Dea, c. 1950s. Photo: Lionel Noble.

Despite the minor delay, I still had to face locomotive inspector Jack O'Dea and explain the whole affair. Jack always asked those awkward questions that made me wonder if I'd get sacked, but he was a good man and I always learned a thing or two from his grilling. In the end, he said I'd done a good job

The Cockburn Line

and, most importantly, had managed to get back into service without a serious delay. He was a hard man, but fair, and back when I was firing for him he always made sure I did my work properly.

I recall one day when I was firing for Jack. We were on the loco pit taking water after cleaning the fire, and I couldn't work out why we weren't getting underway as the guard had already given us the green flag. So I asked Jack what was holding us up. 'I'm waiting for you to put that pricker in its proper position. I don't want it hitting me on the back of the neck,' he said. The pricker was normally placed crossways on two supports on the tender, but I'd put it lengthwise on just one hook. Had questions been asked, I'd have been held accountable for the delay.

Then there was "Y for George", a railway employee in Cockburn. He got that nickname because his first name started with "Y", though everyone mostly just called him George. A New Australian who was clearly lonely, he'd push his bicycle 18 miles to Mingary with an eye for a ganger's wife. One time the ganger, wise to his persistent visits, skipped work to wait for him. When George arrived, an irate man met him and, in no uncertain terms, "brightened" his day by firing bullets from his .303 rifle behind him as he pedalled off back over the rise toward Cockburn.

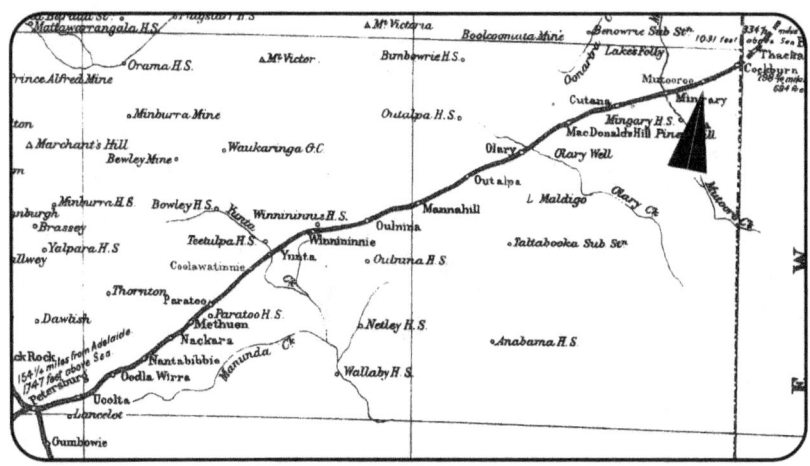

21. Mingary – Mutooroo

Mutooroo was 8¾ miles (14.1 km) from Mingary and 137¾ miles (221.7 km) from Peterborough

Early railway history says that Mutooroo means "good place". Manning's book goes on to say that it was a "railway station, near Olary, aboriginal for 'place of good food.'" Now, while the name suggests good food, you might well ask, 'Where is it?' I often wondered how anyone could live in such an isolated location and why the siding had been placed there at all. Out there, the horizon was nothing but low saltbush with no trees in sight, yet the land supported thousands of sheep producing some of the best wool in Australia.

   The siding opened around 1910 and closed in 1959. Mutooroo sat 621 feet (189.3 m) above sea level, and the scheduled running time from Mingary was 27 minutes on the down and 24 minutes on the up. At the 291-mile mark, just before reaching Mutooroo, there were cottages that were removed in 1930. In 1910, resident ganger Jack Fox and his daughter Lizzie would set off from Mutooroo on a Saturday afternoon on a hand-operated

The Cockburn Line

Mutooroo railway station, c. 1930s. Photo: Lionel Noble Collection.

Remains of the Mutooroo railway yard, c. 1970s. The formation of the passing siding can be seen to the left. Photo: Lionel Noble.

rail trike, headed for Cockburn where Lizzie would spend time with a friend.

Between Mingary Creek and Mutooroo were two level crossings. The first, which was used regularly, allowed vehicle access to nearby sheep stations. The other, at the 289-mile 60-chain mark, was hardly ever used. The posts and the "Look Out for Trains" board eventually rotted away, and nothing was ever done to repair or replace them.

Main steaming on this section kicked in after crossing the wide Mingary Creek (also known as Mosquito Creek) and went on up to the top of the grade at the 286-mile 20-chain mark.

21. Mingary – Mutooroo

From there it was a down grade to Three Mile Creek, then you'd have to steam again to reach the top of a slight grade, and it was easy going until the last bit of steaming into the Mutooroo yard. On the return from Mutooroo, the only heavier steaming was from Three Mile Creek up to that same 286-mile 20-chain rise, and then into Mingary without too much trouble. With Mutooroo at the 292-mile mark, it was an easy section on which to drive or fire. The only time the air brake was needed on an up movement was while running down to the Mingary Creek area from the 286-mile 20-chain point.

Leaving Mingary and looking toward the north side of the line, you'd see large trees near Mingary Creek, the spot where aboriginals once camped in shanties with their dogs. Where they came from or where they headed was always a mystery. But one thing was sure, a toot on the whistle would always prompt them to lift their hands and wave as we passed by.

One day, as we were passing near the second crossing, we suddenly hit a gale-force wind blowing through a narrow corridor. There wasn't much in the way of clouds but that wind, blowing from the south and hitting us side on, almost brought the train to a standstill. The cylinder oil pot perched on the tray above the firebox door was blown straight out of the cab, along with one of our jumpers that had been hanging on the fireman's side. The wind even bent a couple of steel telegraph poles, and a group of trees on the northern side were nearly stripped of leaves. We lost running time because of just how strong that wind was.

The soil in that area was as troublesome as Bay of Biscay; terrible to walk on when it got wet, with mud building up on your shoes. The ground was prone to flooding; water would show up from every direction when it rained. Just a few yards out

The Cockburn Line

Washaway near Mingary, c. 1940s. Photo: Lionel Noble Collection.

Rebuilding the track after flood damage on the Mingary Creek, c. 1950s. Photo: Lionel Noble Collection.

Flood damage at Mingary Creek, c. 1950s. Photo: Lionel Noble Collection.

21. Mingary – Mutooroo

on the Cockburn side, a small culvert always stirred up flood trouble, and further along at the Mingary end the floodwater would wash deep holes under the line.

I was in the area when heavy rain started falling, about 5 inches (127 mm) over a few days. When that much rain came down so fast, it always meant problems. I was working to Cockburn with George Miller when the downpour began. We went into the barracks and got rostered to work on the 600 up, scheduled to depart around 10.00 pm. The weather was still nasty, with lightning flashing in every direction from the town. We left Cockburn, but as we neared the Mutooroo yard, George noticed water right up to the rail head. Feeling uneasy about it, he decided we best stop. He and the guard conferred and spoke to train control, who then instructed us to push back into Cockburn. We signed off duty and headed back to the barracks.

Horse teams work to scoop the ballast back to the track after flooding near Mingary in 1944. Photo: Lionel Noble Collection.

The Cockburn Line

About 24 hours later, in the dark and with the night still stormy, we were sent out on a quad to relieve the crew stranded on the far side of a washaway. The ganger warned us to hold on tight because we were running over sections where the ballast had washed away, leaving holes filled with water that sometimes even flowed. I can still picture the ganger yelling, 'Yahoo!' as we went over a dip, swinging in mid-air on the rails with the sleepers still clinging on. George wasn't too pleased with that kind of frivolity; maybe he was as scared as I was.

That storm held us up for five days. The heavy rain caused 13 washaways along the 18-mile (29 km) stretch between Cockburn and Mingary, though most of the damage was centred on the Mutooroo siding. I recall the very first train through was the express, which derailed over a pig-stied section of the track.

I remember a 1946 flood when I saw fish scattered on the sleepers of the Mingary Creek bridge, the water having topped the bridge and even washed away embankments on both sides. That heavy rain also caused one of the railway dams to burst its banks.

When crews like ours were stranded, we never carried enough money for five days. In those instances, the stationmaster would advance a loan that was later deducted from our wages. Since locomotive crews were paid a food allowance, the department didn't provide us with anything extra unless we were completely isolated where nothing could be bought. Even at a derailment site when the kitchen car (with the cook in charge) was attached to the train, the only thing we could count on was a cup of tea.

Pilot crews on standby at Peterborough for emergencies had to be ready to go immediately. For instance, if they had to travel from Peterborough to Mingary, the department would advise

21. Mingary – Mutooroo

their family, warn them of delays and even get a tucker box of food sent along on the first available train. That sort of thing happened often. And when an accident train was needed, it would pull out right away. In the end, no one starved but we were often inconvenienced for a spell. It wasn't a job to suit everyone; when we went out, we were isolated, often in atrocious weather, and worked long, hard hours.

Engineman George Blyth was known for one particular habit. After leaving Mingary heading toward Cockburn, he'd start rolling a cigarette, a process that seemed to take him forever. By the time he finished, the cigarette had just a few strands of tobacco in it; when he finally lit it, it burned out in a flash with hardly a puff. It was a regular performance and always amusing to watch.

Y-class locomotive 97 on the turntable at the Peterborough loco depot roundhouse, 1967. The Y- and Yx-class were the most used locomotives on the Peterborough Division. Photo: Lionel Noble.

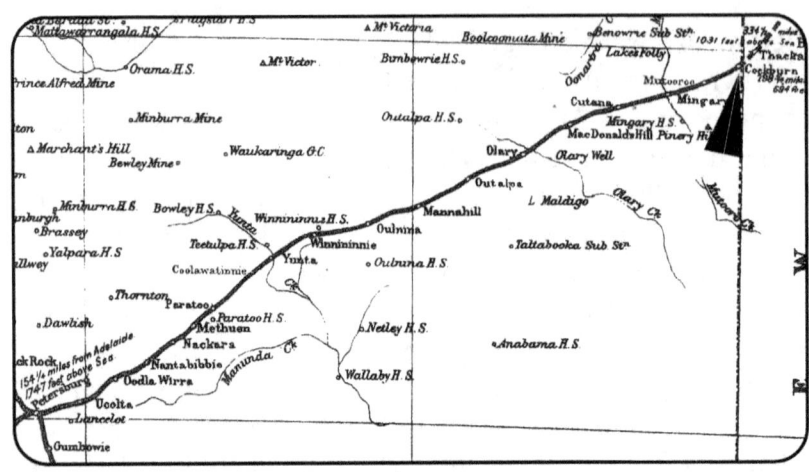

22. Mutooroo – Cockburn

Cockburn was 7¼ miles (11.7 km) from Mutooroo and 145 miles (233.4 km) from Peterborough

Cockburn was named in 1886 after SA premier Sir John Cockburn. Geoffrey Manning's book says, "the town was surveyed by KW Krichauff in 1886, on land held on pastoral lease by William Henry Witting, adjacent to the site of a dam known as Halliday's Dam. Sir John Cockburn (1850–1929), who came to SA in 1875 and settled at Jamestown, was premier in 1889–1890." The railway opened at Cockburn on 14 June 1887 and closed on 10 June 1970. The station was a weatherboard building with the office on the east side, next to a partly covered outdoor waiting area. The railway yard stood 694 feet (211.5 m) above sea level.

The run from Mutooroo to Cockburn was an easy section for the locomotive crew. It involved pulling a slight upgrade after passing over Spielers Creek at the 292-mile 64-chain mark; then light steaming to the first level crossing; a run down over Little Pine Creek Bridge at the 295-mile 42-chain; over Pine Creek

22. Mutooroo – Cockburn

Cockburn railway station, c. 1940. The power plant building is to the far right. Photo: Lionel Noble Collection.

Bridge, the large creek which held up many a train movement at the 295-mile 78-chain mark; over another level crossing; and finally full steaming up to the facing switches at Cockburn. The steepest grade was that last mile into Cockburn. Running times from Mutooroo were about 23 minutes on a down movement and 24 minutes on an up.

There were two level crossings between Mutooroo and Cockburn. The first allowed access to Mundi Mundi Station to the north; the gate for Mutooroo Station was at that same point, but on the opposite side of the Broken Hill road. Andrew Smith, the father of aviators Sirs Ross and Keith Smith, managed Mutooroo Station many years back. The second crossing was at the facing switches just before entering the Cockburn yard, and the level crossing at the eastern end of the yard marked the NSW/SA border.

Pine Creek always seemed to be in flood. It had several openings under the line, yet there wasn't much clearance between the bottom of the bridge and the creek bed. I remember

The Cockburn Line

a time when people feared the bridge might collapse or that water coming from miles away would cover it. Because of the flooding risk, a permanent way employee was stationed on the bank with a small tent for shelter from the sun. His job was to pilot each train over the bridge. One day, as he was reading under the shelter while waiting for the next train movement, a large snake slithered into his little mansion and wound its way up his trouser leg. Luckily, he wasn't bitten. He told me he started using a stool instead and stopped stretching out on the ground.

An insight into flood conditions comes from notes in a 1930s train control record:

> *Pine Creek Rising.*
> *292-mile 60-chains—Floodwater lapping girders.*
> *Lapping girders—284-miles 30-chains bridge. Raining heavily. Gang at bridge.*
> *Casey at 289-mile. Road swinging. Water rising rapidly.*
> *Water over track 274-mile 40-chain.*

On that day, a Tuesday, the express passenger train left Peterborough at 12.55 am, scheduled to arrive at Cockburn at 6.49 am. Floodwaters held it up at Mannahill from 6.15 am until 9.35 am; it arrived at Outalpa on Wednesday at 11.44 am and departed there at 12.05 pm heading back to Peterborough.

Very near the first level crossing, the line passed through the normally dry Lignum Swamp. The swamp, sitting on top of a rise, became especially noticeable after heavy rain. Most of the swamp lay on the southern side of the main road and railway, so the road and line cut through only a small portion of it. Even so, after heavy rains the water lingered for weeks. Before the Broken Hill road was bituminised, the only way for cars and other vehicles to get past Lignum Swamp was to head south for a while, negotiate the lower part of the swamp, then get back onto the main highway. I recall that one night in 1954 as Redex trial

22. Mutooroo – Cockburn

cars were on their way to Broken Hill, 40 points (10.2 mm) of rain fell. Any car that strayed from the road got bogged down, a disaster for many competitors.

In May 1953 after 118 points (29.9 mm) of rain fell at Cockburn, 20 feet (6.1 m) of the railway reservoir's settling pool wall gave way. There had been previous rain at Cockburn—209 points (53.1 mm)—when the road to Olary was covered by 3 feet (0.9 m) of water for two days.

The Cockburn loco depot sat at the northeastern end of the yard. The shed had three lines entering it which, initially, ended as dead ends at the rear but were later extended to the border fence. Firewood for lighting up locomotives was stacked at the rear of the shed. Three locomotive pits were outside the loco shed and others inside ran along its full length. The only building at the rear was the toilets. Tucked into the north-west corner of the shed was the chargeman's office, a modest room with a counter on its east side where the chargeman conducted daily business. Opposite, against the west wall, a wall-mounted desk held the appearance book, where locomotive crews and depot staff signed on and off duty. Booking on at the depot required arrival 25 minutes before train departure, while crews boarding in the traffic yard needed only 10 minutes' notice. Should crews be tasked with preparing their own locomotives, they were allotted 57 minutes. Guards, meanwhile, had 45 minutes to ready a train or just 15 minutes if taking over a prepared unit. General notices filled the west wall of the office, while the shed staff's roster board hung on the outer facade.

On August 13, 1967, a fire ripped through the south-west corner, destroying part of the shed and the adjoining oil store. Although the shed itself was later shortened, the locomotive

> **There had been previous rain at Cockburn—209 points (53.1 mm)—when the road to Olary was covered by 3 feet (0.9 m) of water for two days.**

The Cockburn Line

Early Cockburn loco and traffic yards, c. 1920s. Note the coal stage and coal baskets to the right. The small white building in the centre was the toll house, tolls in the early days having to be paid to cross the border. The butcher shop is behind the overhead tank and the school was adjacent. The house on the corner was the police house which was burnt down in 1906.
Photo: Lionel Noble Collection.

Cockburn loco buildings, c. 1920s.
Photo: Lionel Noble Collection.

22. Mutooroo – Cockburn

*Cockburn loco depot and yard, 1928.
Photo: Lionel Noble Collection.*

*Cockburn railway yard looking toward Mingary, 1939.
Photo: Lionel Noble Collection.*

The Cockburn Line

pits survived. A new oil store was rebuilt near the turntable, preserving the depot's functionality for years to come.

When the depot shed was first built, about 20 equidistant wooden smokestacks protruded from the roof to exhaust locomotive smoke. Each stack was tall, narrow and looked rather odd. After the 1967 fire, the rebuilt shed had only a few stacks as they were no longer needed with the arrival of the 830-class diesel electric locomotives.

The loco foreman's office and store were adjacent to the turntable on the north side of the shed. In 1903, the 45-foot (13.7 m) hand-operated turntable was replaced by a 50-foot (15.2 m) table to take T-class locomotives. Once completed, there wasn't much leeway between the bank surrounds and the foreman's office. Since the turntable was raised above the office, a locomotive risked crashing into the building if it overshot the table.

Cockburn turntable, Loco Foreman's office and old barracks kitchen to the far right, 1972. Photo: Lionel Noble Collection.

A large coal stage was set up to the west of the depot. From there, baskets of coal were tipped onto the locomotive tender. In earlier days a whip was used to swing coal-filled baskets up onto the tender. Engineman Ken Sleep used to say that they had three or four teams of men shovelling the coal. If 40–50 baskets were

22. Mutooroo – Cockburn

Cockburn loco depot prior to the installation of the fuel oil tank, c. 1940s. Photo: Lionel Noble Collection.

Loading coal the old way on a Wx-class locomotive. Coal was loaded using baskets and a whip. Photo: Lionel Noble Collection.

booked on arrival, they'd first shovel the old coal forward on the tender before loading new coal in readiness for the homeward journey.

Initially, the lines within the loco depot led onto the passenger siding, a dangerous arrangement since any vehicles running free from the shed could roll onto the siding, causing damage or loss of life. In later years, when there were at least six lines leading onto the passenger siding, a strict safety routine was established.

The Cockburn Line

By 1936, the Cockburn yard featured four main long shunting lines, one of which carried passenger operations. Two lines branched off toward the west, going over a level crossing to access the stock sidings. A fifth shunting line ran toward a dead end adjacent to the Burns side of the freight shed. All lines were interconnected by switches, giving access to the three border-crossing tracks leading eastwards into the Burns yard in New South Wales—an expansion from the single border-crossing line that had originally served the area. In 1939 moves were commenced to add another line crossing the border. A road crossing doubling as the NSW-SA border, divided the rail sidings of Burns and Cockburn. Trains entering South Australia from Burns were operated by Silverton Tramway Company locomotives, which uncoupled upon arrival, ran "light" through the Cockburn yard and returned to Burns under their own power.

The short dead-end line where the train examiners and undergear repairers worked on defective vehicles was eventually extended, running south of the loco shed to near the border fence. That line couldn't hold more than six vehicles. In 1915, a small gantry was erected on the dead-end for lifting vehicles, and it remained until the end of the narrow gauge era.

Vehicles were often left on the repair line near the loco shed for longer than usual. I recall one night when chargeman Jim Butler watched two drunks staggering over to the loco from the Border Gate Hotel. Laden with packs, they spent quite a while trying to get into a brake van that was sitting unused with one bogie missing. Finally, they settled into one end of the van. Jim walked over, opened the door and said, 'Tickets please.' The pair roused themselves, rummaged through their gear for their tickets and handed them over.

When Jim asked where they were headed, they replied, 'Menindee.'

'Well, you'd better get out and get in the other end,' Jim said. 'This is going to Mingary!'

To get in the other end meant swapping compartments within the same vehicle, and it took those men ages to do the job.

22. Mutooroo – Cockburn

A 25 000-gallon (94 635 L) overhead tank was positioned behind the station building near the large entrance gate on the north side of the station yard. **BURFORD EXHIBITION CANDLES** was printed in bold letters on one side of the tank, the water coming from two reservoirs south of town. Across the road were a butcher, a post office and school on the west end of the street and the police station on the corner.

Railway refreshment rooms were to the rear of the station building. A bell outside these rooms was rung two minutes before the departure time for all passenger trains, and an employee would go in to warn the passengers to take their seats. Before federation, an NSW Customs toll house for border crossings was sited to the east of the refreshment rooms.

In later years, a power shed on the same side as the refreshment rooms housed a diesel engine and generator. Power was only turned on Monday mornings for the ladies of the town

Peterborough engineman Merv Yates (left) and fireman son Robert at Cockburn, c. 1960s. Photo: Lionel Noble.

to do their washing, and again each late afternoon for evening use. It provided a good service, although many times residents still ended up using candles or kerosene lamps.

The large, galvanised iron Cockburn General Store, owned by Arthur Finlay and run in partnership with Bill Hercus,

Finlay and Hercus' shop and boarding house at Cockburn, 1941. Photo: Lionel Noble Collection.

SAR employees out the front of the Cockburn boarding house, 1941. L to R: Tom Swanston, Jack Kelly, Ray Schell, Jim Duffy, Ross Robb, Ron Cook and Allan Duncan. Photo taken at the front of "Hollywood"' Boarding House. Photo: Jack Kelly.

22. Mutooroo – Cockburn

stood on the town's main street. Not far to the south of the store was a small single men's boarding house known by all as Hollywood.

Young enginemen at Peterborough were required to take a turn relieving the Cockburn chargemen for a month at a time. Since we had no cars and no trains to get home to Peterborough on weekends, our wives would send up food each week. I did four such stints when I was a young engineman. The chargeman's job at Cockburn was busy: lighting up locomotives, arranging train departures and crew relief and checking on coal supplies. One of his first duties when a main-line locomotive arrived in the depot was to weigh and replenish the lubricating oil held in two large cylinder pots on the locomotive. That task was extremely important, as cylinder oil went into the sight feed lubricator, while bearing oil was used for the rest of the locomotive. On a normal return trip to Cockburn, about 5 pounds (2.27 kg) of cylinder oil and 7 pounds (3.18 kg) of bearing oil were used.

When the oil-burning locomotives arrived, and before the overhead fuel oil tank was erected, fuelling the locomotives with oil was a problem for the chargeman. The oil was pumped from a rail tanker by a small mobile pump, and it took quite some time to fill a T-class tank. In winter, the fuel oil had the consistency of jelly and wouldn't run, so wooden sleeper fires were lit at ground level along the exposed oil pipe to help warm it up and get it flowing.

The 1918-built railway crew barracks had upper and lower bedrooms, with 12 rooms on each side of each level. Each room had a single bed and about four blankets, which were excellent for winter warmth and very good for sleeping. Initially, we made our own beds, but later the caretaker took over that job. During the summer months, the lower rooms were in great demand because they were cooler.

The lower rooms might have been the coolest, but they also collected every insect that arrived or bred in Cockburn. Green beetle plagues were a nuisance, and some blokes got bitten on their delicate end and suffered for a spell afterwards. Centipedes were a curse if they found their way into your socks. We also had to put up with large, not-so-pretty yellow crickets with long spikes on their tails. Before I went to bed, I'd go in, spray out the mosquitoes, shake out all the blankets and check under the bed. I always hung my clothes up and left my boots and socks on the chair as snakes were also known to wander into those lower rooms now and then.

Cockburn railway barracks, c. 1950s. Sleeping quarters to the left, dining room and kitchen complex centre, bathrooms and toilets to right. Photo: Lionel Noble.

The toilets and two baths in the bathroom had an excellent coke-fired hot water system and were well used. The plentiful, soft dam water was perfect for shaving and bathing, so I often filled the bath and stretched out for a good, long soak. One of the caretakers, a tall fellow named Ted, would often poke his head over the door and ask, 'Having a bath, Lionel?' When he did that, I'd always reply something stupid like, 'No, just peeling some spuds.' What else would you be doing in a full bath with only your head above the water?

22. Mutooroo – Cockburn

The barracks dining room was very large, with 12 or so mostly slate-topped tables. Each man on arriving would claim a table and place his tucker box on it, where it would stay until he left the barracks. No one ever meddled with someone else's box. Off to one side was a large kitchen with a king-size wood stove that provided plenty of heat. Half the time there wasn't enough wood because some of the caretakers were old and didn't have much energy left. I'd watch the men cook meals with repeatedly used fat; the pot, as far as I know, never being emptied. Anything that fell in—something off the ceiling, a cigarette butt or even a blowfly—just stayed there. I didn't touch a bit of it.

Dining room of the Cockburn narrow-gauge barracks, 1966. Employees would leave their tucker box on one of the tables for the duration of their stay. Photo: Lionel Noble.

Two rooms branched off from the dining room. One was the radio/card-game room and the other was the reading room. The card tables could seat six or seven men on each side, and large poker schools were played on weekends when the crews arrived. Some men would play crib, others draughts. One caretaker was a beggar for booze and a pest to those playing cards. He would wander into

The Cockburn Line

the card room, grab hold of the blanket holding the cards and money, and ask, 'Do I get a game or don't I?' The men would then grab their money and wait to see what he'd do. An express guard, arriving around 7.00 am on the Saturday morning express, would sit at that same large table and play poker; he'd only eat biscuits and drink his tea until leaving again at 7.00 am on Monday.

Many footplate men came in and out of the barracks, and in general there was harmony, though every now and then someone under the influence would have a hate session with the rest of the world. Usually, however, there wasn't much time for leisure between day shifts, although weekends afforded a little extra time. On a day shift, by the time we'd cooked our meal on arrival, bathed and then gone to bed, the day had slipped away. We did have at least nine hours off duty, but after an eleven or twelve-hour shift we were just about ready for bed anyway.

There was a barracks paper fund where each man would chip in 3 shillings ($0.30) every now and then to help purchase the Advertiser and other papers that arrived on the paper train around 1.00 am on the day after publication. The money was also used to buy batteries for the Breville radio, which worked well if its battery wasn't flat. Radio was a great companion. When express engineman Fred Hill came in for the weekend, he'd sit with his ear glued to the radio listening to the "Famous Singers" program. He was always a quiet man.

The only telephone in the barracks was in the dining room, connected either to the loco depot or to the station office, each with its own code ring. One old caretaker, Bill Fairclough, was a nice man who always had a smile on his face. Bill was poor of hearing, and when he answered the phone, he'd put the earpiece onto the hearing aid on his chest and always say into the mouthpiece, 'Yes, I am the barracks.'

22. Mutooroo – Cockburn

Another old chap, Jim Patterson, lived in the old barracks by the loco depot and carried all his money in a little pouch around his waist. It was said he wouldn't spend a penny. Jim would hum to himself while working or sitting about, tapping his fingers together. If he had to switch on the light when heading into the bedroom to call a crew member for duty, he'd stand like a shadow and always say, 'Mind your eyes.' Jim was a kind soul.

Cockburn railway barracks caretaker Jim Patterson, 1969. Photo: Lionel Noble.

One of Jim's jobs was to call the crews in time for their shift. One Sunday morning he noticed a message scrawled across the top of the blackboard, "Call all crews in the barracks at 6.30 am Sunday." He failed to notice the small line at the bottom that read, "Account of the Menindee sports' day." Since it was a Sunday, no crews were needed and there wasn't even a sports' day at Menindee. Jim, being the responsible sort who always did as he was told, went ahead and called the crews. After a night at the pub, many of the men ended up wandering around in a daze wondering where their trains were.

One night a mentally unstable fellow wandered into the barracks and challenged some of the men in the dining room to stand up because he claimed he was the king. No one paid him

The Cockburn Line

any mind, so he went into the kitchen where old Jim was doing his usual thing, humming away and keeping in tune with his fingers. Next, he strolled into the room where the pans were kept, picked up a cast-iron pot and banged Jim on the head, nearly killing the poor old bloke. By that time, the others had sensed the visitor's issues and had him pinned down while someone went off to fetch the policeman.

The caretaker's duties were many and varied. He had to keep everything in good order, answer telephone calls, call and advise crews, manage bedding, clean the rooms, service the hot water system, keep the kitchen fire stoked, cut firewood, prepare linen for washing in Adelaide and clean the toilets and bathrooms. With a barracks full of men and a full train service, there was never a dull moment. Later, when caretakers worked under contract, Cockburn's Dulcie Freeman won the job and was loved by all for her kindness to the men.

Dulcie Freeman of Cockburn, 1951. Dulcie and her husband Wally were the caretakers of the Cockburn barracks Photo: D Freeman.

One of the pranks I used to get up to involved my ability to bellow like a cow. When I let out one of my bellowing calls the cows would come running over, and sometimes I'd lead them right into the barracks yard. The men coming back from the hotel would wonder what was going on when they arrived to see

22. Mutooroo – Cockburn

the yard full of cows. Some of the more "pickled" chaps might even have thought they'd wandered into the sale yards. It was all in good fun. One night I even led the cows to the hotel, banged loudly on the front door and then ran off, leaving most of the cows to wander on the veranda.

The night World War II ended, I found myself stuck in Cockburn with engineman Bert Bradtberg and guard Jack Shanahan. Everyone in town was at the hall celebrating but we couldn't join in because we had to work. We were due to depart Cockburn at 10.15 pm but hadn't received any advice about leaving and were anxious to get home. Bert eventually contacted train control and we were told we could leave when we liked. Now, because Jack liked his drinks, the hardest part was getting him moving. We eventually managed to lock him in the brake van and were off. As we passed through various towns along the way, people came out and offered us celebratory food and drink. The oddity was that neither Bert nor I drank, and Jack was still locked in the brake van and didn't come back to himself until we arrived at Nantabibbie. He'd have been fine if he'd had a chance to sleep before leaving Cockburn, so in a way we appreciated that he hadn't objected to us leaving early. I reckon I made a good guard that night. When Jack finally got out at Nantabibbie, he immediately wandered off in the wrong direction, still suffering from the night before. He was a good worker, and later, working in the Peterborough yard as a shunter and shunter's assistant, he performed his job well.

Weekends at Cockburn were spent walking to the reservoirs, occasionally playing tennis, wandering up to the cemetery, reading in the bedroom or listening to the radio if the battery wasn't flat. On Sundays, I'd make myself available to help in the Methodist Sunday School or head over to Ozzie Mercer's place on the north side of town for a singalong. Ozzie's wife was a dear old

> **As we passed through various towns along the way, people came out and offered us celebratory food and drink.**

The Cockburn Line

Cockburn Sunday School students, c. 1950s. Jack Mercer, son of Ozzie Mercer, left front standing next to girl with book in her hand. Photo: Lionel Noble.

soul who would make sandwiches and keep an eye on the girls. Not many respectable young chaps were around in Cockburn, and Mrs Mercer was doing her best to sort us fellows out.

I remember a lad by the name of Bob Abbott who was chasing after one of Ozzie's daughters. At one of the singalongs, Ozzie caught Bob kissing her near the Church of England and he set off after him. Bob managed to get away, but in his stampede he tore his shirt when he got entangled in the barbed wire around the church fence. Ozzie knew what had happened, so the next morning he waited at the loco depot to see who was wearing a torn shirt. Bob, knowing he was being watched, had his mate book him on and ended up leaping onto the engine at the other end of the yard. I never did find out if Ozzie eventually caught up with him.

The highlight of a weekend off at Cockburn was when the South Australian Railways Institute put on a picture show in the institute hall adjoining the Cockburn Hotel. It was a treat to sit on a bench seat with a rug, watching all the local kids and hearing families making a din, all for just 2 shillings ($0.20). The ladies of the town would sell pasties and it made for a good evening.

The first freight train to depart on Monday morning left at 6.55 am. When train examiner Frank Costello returned to the locomotive

22. Mutooroo – Cockburn

after completing the air test, he'd bang on the tender flap with his hammer and say, 'Right driver, you have a full air train and the grade control valves are set in the IP position.' Then he'd turn to the brake van, raise his hand to signal the guard that the test was complete and, as far as he was concerned, the train was ready to go.

Cockburn had three shunt crews working three shifts over a 24-hour period, and when any were on annual leave, relief crews came in from Peterborough. The Cockburn men even went out to relieve the down Peterborough crews when the hours got very long. I remember Percy Murray and Joe Harding being runners-up for the record for time taken between Cockburn and Peterborough with 32 hours on duty, thanks to bad water for the boiler. But Bob Love and Joe Lamb's record of 37 hours still stands as the all-time mark.

> **I remember Percy Murray and Joe Harding being runners-up for the record for time taken between Cockburn and Peterborough with 32 hours on duty, thanks to bad water for the boiler.**

Over the level crossing to the west were the sheep and cattle yards, from where thousands of animals were moved on to Adelaide. The cattle, walked from Queensland for months and fattened along the way, always made for an impressive sight. I enjoyed going down to look at the stock and watch the indigenous drovers manage their horses as they rounded up the cattle. You could even hear the cattle bellowing from the barracks. Since the beasts weren't weighed, the trains were very heavy and behaved differently from other movements, especially when hit by a side wind.

One line to the sheep ramps ran from the passenger line in the station yard, over the level crossing and then split into two lines. The switches for the main line were always left set for the stock yards which was done so that if any vehicle broke loose from the yard it wouldn't end up on the main line. Accidents did happen from breakaway vehicles; I recall one train being

The Cockburn Line

Derailment at Cockburn when the train departed for Mutooroo but the switches were set for the sheep siding, c. 1910. Mrs Eileen Smith in the white dress in the centre of the ladies. Photo: Eileen Smith.

Mrs Eileen Smith (daughter of William Sheerlock of Cockburn) formerly of Cockburn, 1987. Photo: Lionel Noble.

mistakenly sent to the sheep siding. With that steep grade, any loose vehicle would pick up a good speed and run for miles. Engineman Brian McKeough once told me of a string of breakaway vehicles that managed to get all the way to Mutooroo.

Eileen Smith once told the story of a station hand named Bullalinny from Mulyungarie Station who spent his holidays at Cockburn. One time he went over to see a circus train that had arrived in the railway yard. Foolishly, he put his hand in the tiger's cage and it was promptly bitten off. They sent him off to

22. Mutooroo – Cockburn

Broken Hill by train where he was in hospital for many weeks. Mrs Smith said that when he returned, he carried on as normal but with a hook replacing his hand.

Cockburn railway worker Paddy Meaney had a tough time accepting the time given out over the radio, a new invention in his day. Whenever the time was announced, Paddy would grumble, 'That's not right. The time here must be different from Adelaide. It's got to take time to get up here.'

Engineman Tim Jenkins told another story about Paddy.

> *On a Sunday evening during a heat wave, about a dozen of us had been at Cockburn for the weekend and were sitting under the veranda. It had been about 100 degrees (37.8 C) for a fortnight and that day it hit around 108 degrees (42.2 C). No one had had a decent sleep. We were all sitting there, and one chap had been annoying everyone going on about the wonders of the world. No one was interested in what he was talking about, and everybody was wishing he would shut up. We could see a full moon coming up and one of the chaps said, 'Look at that moon. Isn't it a beauty?'*
>
> *'Yes,' replied one of the other men.*
>
> *'Talking about the wonders of the world,' said the annoying man, 'did you know that in America that moon is so powerful that if there was a motor car going across its face you would be able to see it?'*
>
> *Paddy, sitting there with a dirty cigarette butt end hanging off his lip, turned to the chap and said, 'Yes mister, and do you know in America they got a car and if it was going along the face of that moon you would hear the bugger. A joker by the name of Ford made it, and I got one.'*
>
> *Of course, that shut that fellow up altogether. Paddy's car was a model T Ford which he used to take chaps out shooting. It had no bonnet, no windscreen and the seat*

The Cockburn Line

was a piece of board behind the steering wheel. There were quite a few gates to go through on the stations, but Paddy couldn't stop at the gate. He would slowly go up to the gate, put the car into a turn, jump out and open the gate, climb back into the car as it circled back to the gate, go through the gate, set the car circling again while he shut the gate, and then jumped on again as it came past. It was a beautiful thing.

Early railwaymen at Cockburn, c. 1920s.
Photo: Eileen Smith.

23. Cockburn Town

The township of Cockburn was proclaimed on 29 April 1886, but it was with the coming of the railways in 1887 that the town really began. Much of what follows comes from Mrs Eileen Smith of Cockburn, born Annie Eileen Sheerlock on 6 November 1894. Eileen's father, William, bought land in Cockburn and built the first home; by 1891 the town had 56 homes and 206 people.

William Sheerlock, aged 84, the first person to build a house in Cockburn. Photo: Eileen Smith.

In early Cockburn, dugouts with whitewashed walls were everywhere. Later, as proper homes were built, these dugouts were used for storage or to provide a place for single men to board. Mrs Smith mentioned that her family's town lot had two dugouts, one even became a dairy where her mother kept milk

The Cockburn Line

and butter from their 60 cows. Over on the south side near the shop, Arthur "Son" Finlay's block had three or four dugouts.

Eileen's father used his bullock teams with ploughs and scoops to build dams for the government and for surrounding properties, including Lake Dismal, Mutooroo and Burta stations. Mrs Smith wrote:

> [M]y Dad was there before the railway came. He also carted goods from Burra to Broken Hill by bullock wagon before the railway went through. He delivered the first lot of goods to Lot 15 in Broken Hill, which is now the Zinc Corporation, when the mines in Broken Hill first commenced.

Former Cockburn resident Jack O'Callaghan added his recollections of early Cockburn:

> I served two years in the railway at Cockburn, 1915–16. My job was mostly as a 'number nicker' of trucks going to and from the Silverton Tramway Company, where I also learnt Morse telegraph by sound as a hobby. Because of my Morse ability I entered the PMG (post office) department at the start of 1917, where I served for 50 years before retiring in 1965. I knew dozens of railway men along that line, drivers, firemen, guards, etc. I remember pictures I took during the Silverton Tramway strike of camel trains carting wood, chaff and merchandise from Cockburn to Broken Hill. I well remember my railway job. I was doing a man's job and collecting 2 sovereigns every fortnight off the pay train. I was temporary because of a physical defect, according to the railway doctor then, and officially I carried the glorious sounding title of those days, "Glut Junior Porter".
>
> I was scorer for the cricket club, the pitch for which was approximately 100 yards or so parallel to the border fence of NSW behind the loco sheds. The NSW side was called

23. Cockburn Town

Burns. The batsman who drove the ball amongst the gibbers to the fence scored 4. If he hit it over the fence into NSW it was 6.

I remember one horse race meeting. The start was at the rifle range in NSW, and the finishing post was the door of the Border Gate pub, about 50 yards inside the fence in NSW; distance of the race about 4 furlongs. Horses were well into SA when pulled up. Andy Sheerlock, Eileen Sheerlock's brother, rode the winner of the main race with a pair of bike clips around his trouser legs. Rifle shooting and tennis were the two main sports. Weekends were swimming in the railway's stock dam. The town dam was taboo. Kangarooing was another great sport.

Cockburn Sunday afternoon outing, c. 1940. Tom McGaw and Hedley Bray's families, Silverton Tramway employees. Photo: Lionel Noble Collection.

All houses, including Sheerlock's, had dugouts. Lots of young, single railway engine cleaners coming up from the city, used to rent dugouts for a couple of bob ($0.20) a week, or free and batch. Although they were rough old days, I enjoyed every minute of it and, believe me or not,

The Cockburn Line

Finlay's store at Cockburn (rear to left), "Hollywood" boarding house (centre rear) and engineman Arthur Creeper's cottage to left. Photo: Lionel Noble Collection.

Cockburn ladies' Shamrock Cricket Club, 1907-8. Rear (L to R): Mrs Manual, Nellie Stewart, Mrs Knibbs, Mary Sheerlock, Mrs Bessie Jinks, Maud McNamara. Front (L to R): Bessie Manual, Pearl Manual, Ethel Waters, Mrs McNamara, Eileen Sheerlock. Photo: Eileen Smith.

23. Cockburn Town

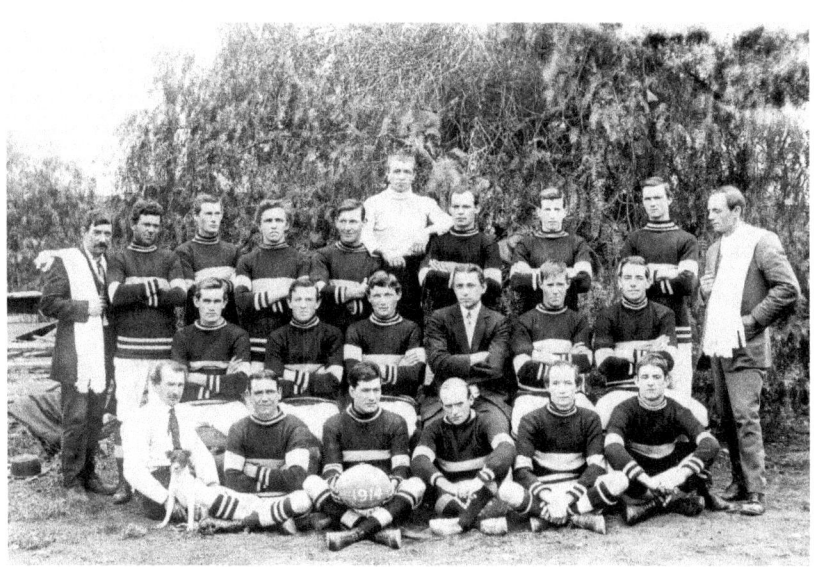

Cockburn Football Club, 1914 (colours chocolate and blue). Front (L to R): Laurie Sheerlock, Jim Madigan, Arnold Waters, Ray Kentish, Bill Peters, _?. Centre (L to R): Douglas Moore, Jack Brennan, George Menz, Post Master, Bill Manual, George Sheerlock. Rear (L to R): _?, Peter Clayton, F Beasley, Barney Fletcher, H Bates, Harry Swanston, Andrew Sheerlock, Arthur Bain, Jim Smith, Jack Sheerlock (trainer). Photo: Eileen Smith.

Cockburn Cricket Club, c. 1935. Sitting (L to R): R Huxtable, W Menz, F Thompson, E Reed. Standing (L to R): J Lynch, S Costello, G Megaw, J Fox, W Hercus, C Ward, J Costello, G Menz, F Costello. Photo: Lionel Noble Collection.

The Cockburn Line

it was the general practice every Sunday afternoon that everyone would dress up in their best clothes and go for walks along the railway line, down around the two railway dams. Strange but true! Now things have changed as I'm told Cockburn is only a railway siding.

A provisional school was established in the town in 1889 with Hannah Miller as the first teacher. The timber-framed, hessian-covered Methodist Church was erected in 1890. Eileen's mother told her that one Sunday a cow poked its head through a hole in the wall. The building was replaced in 1907 with one constructed of wood and galvanised iron. St. Paul's Church of England was opened on 28 February 1908. Eileen and her sister Mary both hammered a nail during the building of that church.

Cockburn Methodist Church, c. 1937. The building was blown down and re-erected using railway lines for support. Mr Bray, Stationmaster for Burns, was Sunday School leader for many years. Photo: Lionel Noble Collection.

The Institute, later to become the Railway's Institute, was erected in 1888. There was a police station, but no records of resident policemen. Mrs Smith recalled:

[M]y earliest recollection of a policeman was Martin Shea, who "arrested" my friend Olive Woods and myself

23. Cockburn Town

and shut us in the gaol as we were on our way to school after lunch. He stood outside the door and enjoyed the joke as we seven-year-olds discussed what reason we could give the teacher, Mr Polson, for being late.

During shearing season at Lake Dismal Station, an Anglican service was held in the shearing shed by the visiting priest from Peterborough. An American harmonium, a reed organ provided and played by Bessie Sheerlock, was used for music. Inevitably, before the notes would produce music, some of the reeds had to be removed with a screwdriver to be cleared of dust particles picked up from the dirt road. Shearers and shed hands of

Cockburn St Peter's Anglican Church, c. 1930s.
Photo: Eileen Smith.

Cockburn main street, c. 1940. Post Office, School, Institute, Hotel.
Photo: Lionel Noble Collection.

The Cockburn Line

all denominations attended the services and joined in the singing of hymns. Seating was on wool bales.

Trains going through to Broken Hill often caused interest to town residents. On one occasion, a huge teapot advertising tea was installed in a truck, while a man standing in the teapot threw out sample packets of tea. Great excitement was caused if a circus was on the train.

"Bundle Mary" was an Assyrian woman who travelled by goods train from Broken Hill to Cockburn every Friday fortnight. She carried a huge bundle of drapery on her back and a baker's basket on her arm. The basket was full of oddments of haberdashery, combs, brushes and china ornaments. She once gave my sister Mary and I a little pink china pig sitting up on its haunches. I often wondered where the pigs went when our old home was dismantled years later.

Sunday afternoon at Cockburn
railway reservoir, c. 1950s.
Photo: Lionel Noble Collection.

23. Cockburn Town

> *Bundle Mary's real name was Mrs Boulas. She was short and stocky in build, and it was a mystery how she could carry such a huge bundle and heavy basket. The bundle contained sheets, tablecloths, pillow slips, fancy covers, clothes, embroidered petticoats, camisoles, bath towels etc. We could hardly wait for the waterproof cover to be taken off the bundle to reveal all the treasures and then be re-packed and tied in knots by the corners. Bunches of shoe and boot laces in black, tan and white were tied on each side of the bundle. It was like a treasure chest to my sister Mary and me. My mother always had a cup of tea ready for Bundle Mary, and our house was her first call after leaving the train in Burns. The train journey took 2 hours, making it a long and tiring day for her. She would leave her home in Crystal Street, Broken Hill, at about 7.00 am or even earlier and it would be 6.30 to 7.00 pm before she would get home again. They had a shop in Crystal Street, where most of the foreigners lived.*

Cockburn was a pleasant, busy place to live in the early days. There was plenty of activity in the town and on the railway. Many buildings no longer exist now that the narrow-gauge era has ended. Sundays were reserved for a walk out to the railway reservoir and catchment, and I was always lucky if I could score a ride to Broken Hill for the weekend. Long before I was married, Bill Hercus and Arthur Finlay took me to a boxing show in Broken Hill on a Saturday evening. Sometimes I'd catch a ride on the Sunday Mail truck to Broken Hill. It would arrive from Adelaide in the early hours of Sunday morning, then I'd sit in darkness on bundles of newspapers, covered in dust and freezing cold as the truck made its long, boring trip to Broken Hill. I'd return on the first train early on Monday, then work my way home to Peterborough after lunch. And if I encountered a stubborn truck driver who wouldn't cooperate, I'd simply go back to bed.

24. A Cockburn Stationmaster

The life of a stationmaster at any siding, especially in the country, was busy. You were expected to be everything from a bank advisor, town organiser, income tax consultant and even a marriage guidance counsellor, all in addition to your railway duties. Kenneth Moody was born on 4 July 1921 at Denial Bay, South Australia, the youngest son and second youngest of nine children. I'm pleased to share the following memoir of his three years as Cockburn stationmaster.

> *I was educated at Bonython Primary School and then at the Ceduna Higher Primary School, obtaining an intermediate certificate in seven commercial subjects. I began my working career helping to clean wheat with a hand-powered winnower, sewing up bags of grain, drawing water from the underground storage tanks for livestock and, when possible, working on the wharf at Thevenard as a labourer. My wife and I arrived at Cockburn on 26 November 1953, and we eventually left on 26 November 1956.*
>
> *Over a period at Cockburn, junior clerk Deane Klinger and I were the only two Australian-born employees on the transportation staff. The others, including a clerk, two shunters and porters, were Greek, German, Italian and Yugoslav immigrants who didn't always get on with one another. I was called in one night to settle a difference between an Italian and a German. The German, carrying a .303 rifle, was threatening to shoot the Italian, who said he would call the stationmaster—me! The German said he would shoot him too. The Italian said he would call the*

24. A Cockburn Stationmaster

police, only to be told by the irate German that he would shoot them too. The German didn't turn up for his shift that night and I had to do it for him. The trouble seemed to have been caused by some heavy drinking and resulted in the German being suspended from duty for two days and cautioned for the incident.

On another occasion I asked a rather rugged type of guard how he got his shiner (severely blackened eye). Enquiries revealed that the guard had an altercation with a smaller, lightly built fireman who was resting while off duty in the local barracks. Apparently, the guard's braces broke during the fight which, with his fallen trousers effectively hobbling him, enabled the fireman to take full advantage and get revenge.

While stationed at Cockburn, any railway staff willing to help were encouraged to clear surroundings, repair back-stops on the two railway tennis courts and to top dress the surfaces with material supplied mainly through the SA Railways Institute. Around 1954, the Cockburn Institute Hall was vested in the hands of the local committee of the SA Railways Institute. Loco foreman, Jesse Averis, provided jacks and equipment to set up steel uprights and insert crossbeams to straighten and align the leaning building. The floor was in reasonable condition. The piano was sent to Adelaide for tuning, an attention which proved ineffective, so amplified recorded music was provided for periodic dances and functions.

Second-hand cricket bats, balls, wickets and coconut matting used for concrete pitches were stored in the Institute. Cricket bat handles and blades were inserted as necessary by the Adelaide Sports Depot through the Adelaide Railways Institute. The cricket club was re-formed, and arrangements were made to play one-day Sunday cricket matches against the Broken Hill Postal

The Cockburn Line

Institute and the Silverton Railways. Several Broken Hill teams were then sponsored by Broken Hill hotels.

During normal weekends three Peterborough train crews would rest in the Cockburn railway barracks. By contacting the Peterborough rosterman on Fridays, it was possible to obtain the names of two or three enginemen, firemen or guards who could be utilised to supplement and strengthen our Sunday cricket teams. Such names as Gordon Jeffs, Luke and Marty Brennan, George Harper, Ted White, Stan Bungey, Murray Chandler, Ross "Dusty" Roads, Kevin and "Snow" Norman and Bob Weekly readily come to mind. The Peterborough men were keen to play, as quite often the Broken Hill teams awarded small incentive trophies for the best opposing batsman, bowler and fielder.

About 1954, Laurie Ryan was appointed Cockburn loco foreman, replacing Jesse Averis who was promoted and transferred to Port Lincoln. Brian Kelley was appointed Cockburn station clerk in 1955. Laurie and Brian were very good country cricketers and strengthened our cricket team so much that the Broken Hill teams became reluctant to play us. When we last played the postal institute team at Broken Hill for the annual cricket cup trophy, they apparently considered our team to be stacked and didn't surrender the trophy.

Around 1955, Radium Hill sought a competitive cricket team and, as there was a SA Highway's camp and a SA Railways relay gang stationed at Olary, an official three-team association was formed to play one-day Sunday cricket matches between Cockburn, Olary and Radium Hill. We were playing cricket about 11.00 am one Sunday at Olary. A dust storm was raging and Laurie Ryan, who was fielding in slips, complained that he couldn't see the bowler at the opposite end coming in to bowl. The match still went on.

24. A Cockburn Stationmaster

Cockburn Cricket Club, 1954-55. Front (L to R): Murray Lubke, Alf Rutherford, Peter Butler, Perce Freeman, Bill Place. Standing (L to R): Allan Gilbert, Brian Rutherford, Phil Marshall, Dan Minahan (umpire), Ken Moody (capt), Jim Snow, Bruce Norman, Kevin Jackaman. Photo: K Moody.

As president of the Olary–Cockburn–Radium Hill Cricket Association, I attended a delegates' weekend night meeting at the Radium Hill Hotel. I sat down in a comfortable chair in the hotel lounge but was politely informed that the chair was reserved for the local unlicensed SP bookmaker. I promptly vacated. About three weeks later, police detectives from Port Pirie arrived and one whom occupied the same comfortable chair was given the same information. The detective obliged and shifted, but of course it wasn't long before the SP bookmaker came, occupied the chair and was apprehended and dealt with.

Around 1955, the Cockburn cricket oval was graded and goal posts erected to enable a few Sunday games of football. It was difficult to obtain numbers though people were also sought from nearby sheep stations. In 1956, a nine-hole golf course was laid out near the

The Cockburn Line

railway dam and catchment area, and a second-hand steel railway carriage for a club room was obtained from Islington and transported to the site by local carrier, Alan Wastell.

In October 1956, about five weeks after water from the railway settling pool had been drained into the railway dam, I remember seeing a mass of blue-grey kangaroos grazing on the lush vegetation of the settling pool area. When kangaroos were feeding, their heads, backs and tails would come into view, giving a false impression of numbers. In this instance I systematically counted at least sixty kangaroos in the mob, a number which I think was very unusual and almost unbelievable.

From 1953 to 1956, I was secretary/treasurer of the Cockburn Children's Christmas Tree Fund. The fund originally catered for children of local SAR employees, children from the Burns Silverton Tramway and children of a few town residents. The number of recipient children was increased from one hundred to two hundred when it was decided to include the children of employees from Mutooroo, Mulyungarie, Pine Creek and Thackaringa sheep stations. Our local shopkeeper, Bill Hercus, used to permit the wives of local families to use his wholesale account in Adelaide warehouses to obtain toys and gifts for children. It was a great concession for the children and was very much appreciated. Mutooroo Station organised a large wool shed barn dance and provided a dance band and sumptuous supper for the benefit of the Christmas Tree parents.

I retired on 26 June 1986, after attaining over 46 years of continuous service. I worked in all four divisions of the South Australian Railways and was stationed in 16 different stations and/or locations. I relieved and/or worked at all country and suburban ticket office windows. In all, I worked in at least 63 different stations during my railway career.

25. Closing Thoughts

As far back as I can remember, locomotives were a fascination to me. As a child in my Queensland birthplace of Wondai, I apparently unlawfully spent time in the small railway yard there. The Wondai stationmaster would send the porter to my father's house, telling him, 'Keep your boy out of the railway yard.'

When I was 7 years of age, we moved to High Wycombe, Bucks, England. Tracks running to various places in the north of England passed behind our house, and I would poke sticks in the ground and mimic the signalman in his box by moving the sticks after he moved the signal lever. Even at the school I attended, trains ran along a high embankment for the full length of the school yard. Once someone presented me with a toy Hornby clockwork train set, complete with two levers with small brass knobs in the locomotive cabin. After winding up the interior spring with a heavy key, the two levers made the machine go forward or reverse.

Returning as a 9-year-old in 1934 to Australia, my family settled in Peterborough where there were more trains to watch! There were also scrapped locomotives and vehicles to play on just outside of Peterborough near the cemetery; and then my eldest sister married a locomotive fireman. It's no wonder that my love for railways only grew as I got older.

There always seemed to be something happening on the Peterborough Division. Troop trains during the war, coal trains, Commonwealth locomotives being serviced in the workshops, Silverton Tramway Company locomotives on loan to the Division, the arrival of the 300- and 400-class locomotives and newly built locomotives for other systems passing through.

The Cockburn Line

Post-war, it was expected the amount of work would reduce with fewer men required. While the troop trains stopped, the Leigh Creek coal trains were a real boost as they replaced the troop trains and created even more trains and more work. Then came the diesels, which required fewer men and halved the workload due to longer consists. Dieselisation was followed by standardisation, a fascinating time for me as it involved a great deal of reorganising and training.

Although it's difficult to describe, there was always a special bond between the two men on the locomotive. I quickly noted it, adapted to it and it stayed with me for the rest of my footplate life. While we leaned on and learned to trust each other, it wasn't always so; some men simply couldn't work together because of personality clashes. I saw it happen at times between two men paired for work, so they were split and given new workmates. Generally, though, the comradeship was something special. It was disappointing to see that spirit disappear when diesel locomotives arrived, as there wasn't that same individual challenge for the fireman or engineman. Both positions changed, a change which took its toll on man and job.

The happiest of all my footplate working days were spent on the Peterborough Division. There were so many early enginemen with whom I worked at Cockburn, Port Pirie, Quorn or Terowie, men who helped me grow in my job as a fireman and engineman. It was a pleasure to be rostered with them. Some passed on to their eternal reward long before retirement or only lived a short while after retiring. It always made me sad; it seemed they were jilted after giving so much of their lives to the department. They had worked in appallingly primitive conditions ever since their start on the footplate. I never felt as hard pressed as some of those earlier men who turned the wheels on the system with pride and determination.

25. Closing Thoughts

I'm so pleased to have been involved in some way as a fireman, engineman, instructor, running shift foreman and finally locomotive inspector. I always found it a delight to go to work. Every moment was a challenge; every day something different happened. My original love of locomotives and trains has never waned. At this stage in my life, I couldn't be bothered to learn once again about the Stephenson valve gear, in or outside admission valves, pear-shaped grooves, cut-away corners and equalising ports; nor could I be bothered with whether the brake pipe pressure exceeded the main reservoir pressure or if there were two bricks missing from the arch. But I'm certain that, given the opportunity, I'd do it all again starting from the time checker's office at the Peterborough locomotive depot, just as I did in March 1944 when I transferred from the Mile End depot.

Lionel died aged 90 in September 2015 at Bethsalem Nursing Home, Happy Valley South Australia.

Editor's Acknowledgements

My thanks go to the following people who helped to make this edition possible.

Nancy Jackson for her helpful suggestions and careful editing (any residual mistakes are mine).

Those who took the time to read the manuscript and offer feedback: Bob Yates, John Schell, Bob Hams, Peter Caunce, John Evans, Doug and Judy Evans, Gordon Crabb, Kym Boxall.

Bob Hammond and Mark Carter of the National Rail Museum in Port Adelaide for their encouragement and willing assistance.

Jason Schell of Steamtown Peterborough for his encouragement and assistance.

Those who have given permission for the use of photographs: Helen Blake (Rasmus family), Murray Billett, Australian Railway Historical Society of NSW (Alex Grunbach), National Rail Museum Port Adelaide.

My wife Wendy who always encourages me and who does a creditable job of appearing interested as I describe the latest issue I've had to try and solve with the typesetting software.

Bibliography

Day, Alfred (compiler), *Names of South Australian Railway Stations with Their Meanings and Derivations* (Adelaide: REE Rogers, Government Printer, 1915)

Manning, Geoffrey H, *Manning's Place Names of South Australia* (Modbury: Gould Books, 2006)

Venus, R, *Steamtown Heritage Rail Centre* (2017, Engineers Australia, Engineering Heritage SA) https://portal.engineersaustralia.org.au/system/files/engineering-heritage-australia/nomination-title/HRP.Steamtown Peterbrouugh.Nomination and report.V2.15 Nov 2017.pdf

Index

A
Aboriginal. See Indigenous
Abottomey, Mr 43
Accident 48, 56, 116, 131, 134, 173
Acocia Creek 128
Adelaide 1, 3, 12, 38, 57, 94, 125–126, 130, 132, 170, 173, 175, 185, 187, 190, 195
Adelaide Museum 38
Aeroplane 9–10, 101
Aircraft. See Aeroplane
Alszko, Mrs 67
Altman, Jack 127
Andrews, Nancy vi
Andrews, Stan vi, 104, 114–115
Asher, Jack 105
Australian Army 3, 59
Australians, New 19, 146, 186
Averis, Jesse 187–188

B
Bain, Arthur 118, 181
Ballast 34, 44, 74, 76–77, 90, 98, 113, 125, 129, 137, 151–152
Barracks 98, 110
Bates, H 181
Beasley, F 181
Bettison, Ken 82–83
Bicycle 7–8, 15, 48, 131, 146
Billett, Murray 81
Bishop, George vi
Blyth, George 78, 153
Boer War 58
Boilermaker 36, 99
Bond, Jack 137–138
Bonython Primary School 186
Boolcoomatta Pastoral Station 134
Borbas, John 117
Boulas, Mrs (Bundle Mary) 184–185
Bradshaw, Dave 135
Bradtberg, Bert vi, 171

Brake Van 20, 32, 50, 98, 105, 116–117, 131–132, 143, 162, 171, 173
    Dolly Varden 143
Brant, B 115
Bray, Hedley 179
Brennan, Dan vi, 14, 55, 96
Brennan, Jack vi, 181
Brennan, Luke 188
Brennan, Martin 188
Bridge 33, 43, 68, 75, 79, 82, 93, 101–102, 105–107, 112, 114, 122, 135, 137, 139–140, 152, 154–156
Broad Gauge 1, 130
Broken Hill 1–3, 12, 16, 27, 40–41, 48, 58, 61, 66, 82, 94, 101, 106, 109, 111, 113, 121, 125, 127, 130–131, 134–135, 141, 155–157, 175, 178, 184–185, 187–188
Broken Hill Express 12, 16, 69, 105, 107, 131, 156, 168
Broken Hill Postal Institute 187–188
Brooks, Joseph (early surveyor) 18, 27, 121
Broom 51, 82, 145
Buick, Frank 134
Bullalinny 174
Bullock 31–32, 82, 91, 178
Bulloo Creek Pastoral Station 134
Bundle Mary. See Boulas, Mrs (Bundle Mary)
Bungey, Stan 188
Burford Exhibition Candles 163
Burns 12, 162, 179, 182, 185, 190
Burra 69, 178
Burta Pastoral Station (NSW) 178
Butler, Jim 162
Butler, Peter 189

C
Camaraderie. See Comradeship
Camel Team 142, 178
Camp 42–43, 70, 94, 119, 125, 140, 149,

188
Capitol Theatre 106
Cartwright Pastoral Station 128
   Dams 128, 131
Casey Jones. See Ganger, Railway, Quad
Casey, Bill 'Boof' 55
Casey, Howard 115
Casey, Mick 43
Cattle 77. See Also Stock
Ceduna 186
Cemetery 27–28, 171, 191
Centipedes 144, 165
Central Australia 2
Chaff 44, 178
Chamberlayne, Lloyd 86
Chambers, William 65, 69–70
Chandler, Murray 188
Changi 120
Chargeman, Railway 157, 162, 165
China 74
Christmas 16, 94, 190
Circus Train 174, 184
Clayson, Les 70
Clayton, Peter 181
Cleaner, Railway 3, 14–15, 179
Coal 7–9, 18, 36, 47, 52, 54, 64–65, 69, 78, 80–82, 85, 145, 158, 160–161, 165, 191–192
   Basket 64, 145, 158, 160–161, 184
Cockburn vi, 2, 5, 12–13, 15–17, 19–20, 23, 32, 36, 53, 55–56, 64–65, 70, 77, 79, 84, 89–90, 93, 99, 117–119, 126–127, 131–133, 137, 142–146, 148, 151–159, 161–167, 169, 171–190, 192
   Barracks 107, 124, 131, 151, 165–170, 173, 187–188
      Breville Radio 168, 171
      Caretaker 165–170
      Green Beetle Plagues 165
      Paper Fund 168
      Poker Games 107, 167–168
   Boarding House 164–165, 177, 180
   Border Gate Hotel 124, 162, 179
   Butcher 158
   Church of England 172, 182–183
   Cockburn Hotel 183
      Hotel 172
   Cricket 178, 180–182, 187–189
   Dugouts 177–179
   Football 181
   Height Above Sea Level 154
   Institute 19, 172, 182–183, 187
   Loco Depot 157–162, 165, 168–169, 172, 178
   Methodist Church 171, 182
   Naming of 154
   Picture Show 172
   Police 158, 163, 170, 182, 187
   Railway Station 155, 163
      Refreshment Rooms 163
   Railway Yard 154–155, 157–160, 162–163, 172–174
      Coal Stage 160
      Oil Tank 161
      Power Shed 163
      Toll House 158, 163
   Reservoir 157, 163, 171, 179, 184–185, 190
   School 158
The Cockburn Line iv–vii, 12–13, 16, 23, 29, 33, 36, 65–66, 71, 75, 80, 91, 99–100, 103–104, 108, 112–113, 116, 121, 126, 133, 139
   Line Closure 12
Cockburn, Sir John 154
Coffey, Jack 125
Coglin, Micky 69
Cold 56, 105, 125, 185
Commonwealth 191
Comradeship 10, 85–86, 90, 108, 170, 192
Cook, Les vi, 107
Cook, Ron 164
Coolawatinnie 61, 65–68, 71–72, 75–76
   Dead Man's Hill 69–70
   Height Above Sea Level 68
   Railway Station 68
   Railway Yard 68
Coombe, Mr 72
Cooper, Mr 133
Cornwell, Bob 24
Costello, Frank 172, 181
Costello, J 181
Costello, S 181
Cottages, Railway 14, 21, 23–24, 33, 49, 61, 66, 74–75, 79, 96–98, 107–108, 111, 122, 128–129, 135–136, 141, 144, 147, 180
Cows 34, 50, 77–78, 170–171, 178, 182
Crane 9, 74
Cream 50

Creeper, Arthur vi, 180
Crew Relief 32, 66, 118, 141, 165, 173
Cricket 178, 180–181, 187–189
Crossing, Railway Level 6–7, 13–14, 17, 20, 22–23, 27, 40–41, 48–49, 58, 61, 68–69, 75, 80, 89, 93–94, 101–102, 106, 111, 121–122, 125, 127–128, 134–135, 148–149, 154–156, 162, 173
Crow 90
Culvert 43, 76, 107, 125, 137–138, 151
Cummings, Blanche 22
Cutana 17, 111, 113, 116, 121–123, 125, 127–128, 130–131, 133–134, 137, 139–142
   Height Above Sea Level 128
   Naming of 128
   Railway Station 128–129
   Railway Yard 128–130, 138

D

Daley 32, 109
Dann, Alf 27, 34
Davidson, T 115
Dead Man's Hill. See Coolawatinnie, Dead Man's Hill
Denial Bay 186
Depression, Great 140
Derailment 56, 69, 99, 105, 113–114, 137, 143–144, 152, 174
Diamantis, Paul 98
Dickson, Alf 90
Dieselisation 192
Diplodocus 38
Dodman, Bob 15
Dowd's Hill Tunnel. See Ucolta, Dowd's Hill Tunnel
Drew's Well 26
Drinking Water 36, 44
Drought 43, 66
Duchoslav, J 39
Dueter, Joe 139
Duffield 111
Duffy, Jim 164
Duncan, Allan 164
Dunk, R 115
Dust Storm iii, 96, 104, 188

E

Eckert, Fred 91
Electric Staff 24, 40, 59–60, 63, 65, 68, 90, 98, 100, 108, 121, 123, 125, 127, 131
Engineman, Railway 3, 8–15, 19–20, 22, 24, 30, 33, 36, 38, 43, 45, 48, 51, 53, 55–56, 59, 61, 66, 69, 76–78, 81–82, 85, 91, 96–99, 102, 105–108, 113, 117–118, 123, 125–127, 136–137, 140, 142–143, 153, 160, 163, 165, 168, 171, 174–175, 180, 192–193
Estonia 19
Eurelia 46, 66, 98
Evans, K 39
Evans, WO 9
Examinations 3, 38
Examiner, Train 36, 78, 84, 93, 116, 162, 172

F

Fairclough, Bill 168
Fenwick, Bill 107
Fettler, Railway 66
Finlay, Arthur 164, 178, 180, 185
Fire 30, 157, 160, 165
Fireman, Railway 3, 12–13, 15, 18–20, 22, 24, 30, 36–40, 43–45, 47, 50–53, 55–56, 58, 65, 69, 71, 75–78, 80–82, 84, 86, 90, 92, 96–98, 100, 105, 108, 113, 117–120, 123–125, 127, 131–132, 137, 142, 144–146, 149, 163, 178, 187–188, 191–193
Firewood 31–32, 41, 157, 170, 178
Fish 152
Fitzgerald 32, 67, 90, 123
Flaman Speed Recorder 130
Fletcher, Barney 181
Floods iii, 18, 20, 33–34, 75–76, 82, 90, 106–107, 112–113, 125, 130, 137, 140, 149–152, 155–156
Flour Mill 32
Food Allowance 152
Football 45, 181, 189
Foote 102
Footplate Men 12, 14, 43, 168
Ford, Model T 175
Foreman, Railway 43, 110, 112
Foreman, Railway District 114–115
Foreman, Railway Loco 77, 132, 134, 160, 187–188
Foreman, Railway Running Shift 14, 51, 77, 193
Fox 92
Fox, Jack 147, 181

Fox, Lizzie 147
Freeman, Dulcie vi, 15, 170, 189
Freeman, Percy 189
Freer, Jack 139
Freight Shed 65, 73–74, 79, 162
Freight Spur Lines 41, 56, 74, 114
Freight Train 23–24, 30, 45, 47, 58, 89, 92, 102, 118, 122, 172
Fuel 10, 16, 69, 145, 161, 165

G
Ganger, Railway 34, 36, 39, 42–43, 49, 64, 70, 104, 107, 112, 114–115, 121, 125, 130–131, 134, 139–142, 144, 146–147, 152, 156, 188
    Flying Gang 124–125
    Quad 134, 144–145, 152
Generator 74, 163
German, Germany 19, 37, 186–187
Gilbert, Allan 189
Gladstone 1, 36
Gold 106
Goods Train 16, 109, 137, 184
Govette, Vincent 127
Grasshoppers 24, 35, 43, 127
Great Northern Line 1, 124
Greek 186
Grunbach, Alex vi, 35, 62, 122
Guard, Railway 6, 22, 37, 65, 69, 76, 82, 85–86, 97, 105, 107, 109, 117–119, 123, 125, 127, 131, 137, 142–144, 146, 151, 157, 168, 171, 173, 178, 187–188
Gum Creek 122. See Also Olary Creek
Gumbowie 18, 20

H
Haddrill, Ivan 115
Hall's Well 98–99
Hallet, J 79
Halliday's Dam 154
Hambly, Jack 90–91
Hams, Bob 51, 113
Hanlon, Harry vi, 56
Harding, Joe 'Paddy' vi, 98, 137–140, 144, 173
Harmonium 183
Harper, George 188
Harrold 111
Hawes, Victor 85
Heat 69, 124–125, 167, 175

Heithersay, John 35
Hercus, Bill 164, 181, 185, 190
Herde 102
High Wycombe 191
Highway's Department 188
Hill and Co. 141
Hill, Fred 14, 168
Hillgrange 41
Hocking, Colin 96
Hocking, V 115
Hogg, Roy 22, 131
Horses 34–35, 70, 98, 125, 134, 141, 173, 179
    Horse Teams 32, 44, 46, 69, 104, 142, 151
Howard, Chris 31
Hucks, Ben 32–34, 42–44, 46, 49
Hucks, Edie 33
Hucks, May 34
Humpy 40, 43–44, 66, 100, 108, 118, 121, 125–126, 130–131
Hurd 111
Hutton's Lagoon 14, 28–30, 33
Huxtable, R 181

I
Indigenous 18, 27, 40, 47, 72, 133, 147, 149, 173
Inglis, Jock 107
Institute, SA Railways 19, 172, 182–183, 187
Islington 190
Italian 186

J
Jackaman, Kevin 189
Jackson, N 39
Jacobs 28
Jacobs Creek 94
Jamestown 142, 154
Jedrich, Joe 97
Jeffs, Gordon 188
Jenkins, Tim vi, 13–14, 20, 61, 66, 76, 119, 175
Jinks, Bessie 180
Jock the Fireman 123
Johnston 53
Jordan, Bill 'Brumby' 8, 108
Jumbuck Creek 94

K

Kaehne, Wally 137–138
Kamin, Ron 69
Kangaroos 27, 40, 44, 49, 61, 71, 128, 131, 179, 190
Kelley, Brian 188
Kelly, Jack 142–144, 164
Kendell, Jim 42–43
Kentish, Ray 181
Klinger, Deane 186
Knibbs, Mrs 180
Koch, Heine 10
Kosh, Jack 40
Krichauff, KW 154
Kuester, W 76

L

Lafestry, Cliff 107
Lake Dismal Pastoral Station 178, 183
Lamb, Joe 173
Lancelot 30
Lead (metal) 109, 135
Lectures 3
Leigh Creek 192
Lignum Swamp 156
Lillywhite, Dave 59, 86, 97
Limestone Siding 109
Lively, Harry 114
Loch Lilly Pastoral Station 104
Locomotive Inspector 11, 38, 78, 113, 132, 145, 193
Locomotive Instructor 193
Locomotives
    300-class 76, 92, 116–117, 125–126, 136, 191
    400-class 38, 50, 53, 69, 77, 82–83, 92, 97, 191
    600-class 28, 129, 140
    830-class 50, 101, 160
    Air Brake 8, 30, 38, 51, 81, 124, 141, 144, 149, 173
    Ash Pan 36, 170
    Axle 19, 82, 84, 126
    Bearing Oil 165
    Blast Pipe 53–54
    Blow-off-cock 54
    Boiler 9, 19, 47, 50, 52, 54, 61, 80, 85, 99, 122–123, 125, 144, 173
    Boiler Flues 53–54
    Boiler Tubes 53–54, 66, 132
    Breakdown iii, 82, 84, 142
    Cinders 54
    Clinker 36, 54
    Connecting Rod 71, 76, 84, 116
    Cowcatcher 20, 25
    Crosshead 76, 84–85
    Cylinder Oil 11, 149, 165
    Double Header 28, 66
    Eccentric Rod 76, 99
    Fire 6, 30, 36, 50, 52, 54, 60–61, 65, 78, 81, 85, 90, 108, 144, 146
    Firebox 18–19, 36, 51–52, 54, 67, 80, 85, 125–126, 132, 145, 149
    Firebox Grate 36
    Footplate 44, 76–77, 84–85, 192
    Funnel 50, 52–54, 80, 122–123, 126
    Gauge Glass 19–20, 54, 59
    Grease Pack 126
    Gudgeon Pin 85
    Hand Brake 30, 45
    Headlight 21, 127
    Hot Bearing 126
    Injector 52
    Jacks 83, 137, 187
    Jimmy 53–54
    Lighting Up 157, 165
    Lubricating Oil 165
    Mechanical Lubricator 85
    Oil-Burning 9, 114, 165
    Petticoat Cowl 53
    Piston 54, 76, 84
    Pit Work 6, 9, 36, 50, 54, 61, 77–78, 84–85, 99, 126, 146
    Pony Wheel 82–84
    Priming 50, 116
    Regulator 30, 36, 38, 54, 134
    Reversing Gear Lever 36, 81
    Sand Box 35–36, 114
    Smoke Box 53–54, 77
    Spark Arrester 54
    Steam/Steaming 18–20, 28, 47, 50, 52–55, 58, 60, 75–76, 80, 84–85, 89, 92–93, 100, 116, 120, 122–123, 130, 134, 145, 148–149, 154–155
    Steam/Steaming Light 60, 75, 83, 93, 100, 122, 130, 154, 162
    Steaming Efficiency 53, 80
    Syringe (water) 19
    T-class ix, 12, 21, 30, 38, 52, 59, 64, 84–85, 98–99, 130, 137, 160, 165

Tender 6, 13, 19, 21, 25, 30, 36, 38, 45, 51, 64, 67, 77–78, 81, 90, 116, 125, 127, 137–139, 145–146, 160–161, 173
V-class 8
Valve 54, 76, 84, 117, 123, 127, 134, 145, 173, 193
Whistle 20, 22, 38, 48, 66, 96, 149
White Feather Flying 123–124
Wx-class 161
X-head 85
Y-class 48, 153
Yx-class 15, 153
Love, Bob 173
Lubke, Alf 189
Lux Creek 128
Lynch, J 181

M

Madex, Neville 132
Madigan, Jim 181
Malycha, Mrs 22
Mann, C 117
Mannahill ix, 16–17, 53, 92–94, 96, 98–102, 104–105, 108, 114, 134, 156
   Height Above Sea Level 93
   Mannahill Hotel 98
   Naming of 93
   Railway Station 93–95
   Railway Yard 94, 96–99, 101
   Reservoir 94, 98
Manning, Geoffrey 27, 47, 89, 133, 147, 154
Manual, Bessie 180
Manual, Bill 181
Manual, Mrs 180
Manual, Pearl 180
Marshall, Phil 189
Marsland, Stan 139
Matthews, Fred 97
Maxwell, Miss 140
McCabe, Tom 31
McDonald 76
McDonald's Hill 17, 118, 121–128, 130–131
   Naming of 121
   Railway Station 122
   Railway Yard 121–122, 126–127
McGaw, Tom 179
McKay, Jack 22
McKeough, Brian 174
McKeough, Jim vi
McNamara, Maud 180
McNamara, Mrs 180
McPherson, Bruce 37, 69
Meadow Downs Pastoral Station 34
Meadows, George 53
Meadows, W vi
Meaney, Paddy 175–176
Medlin, Jack 31
Megaw, G 181
Menindee 162, 169
Menz, George 181
Menz, W 181
Mercer 43, 48
Mercer, Jack 172
Mercer, Mrs 172
Mercer, Ozzie 171–172
Mesecke, Harold vi, 14, 43
Methuen 17, 49, 54, 58–60, 65–66
   Height Above Sea Level 58
   Naming of 58
   Railway Yard 58
   Siding 59
   Station 58–59
Meyer, Pastor 72
Middleton, Phil 137–139
Mile End 3, 193
Milk 34, 50, 92, 177
Miller George 'Catta' vi, 14–15, 38, 53, 69, 104, 131, 142–144, 151
Miller, Hannah 182
Minahan, Dan 189
Mingary 17, 127–128, 132–135, 138, 140–147, 149–153, 159, 162
   Height Above Sea Level 133
   Naming of 133
   Railway Station 133–134
   Railway Yard 134, 136, 141
      Koolka Siding 135
      Siding 144
   Reservoir 135, 141–142
   Stationmaster 141
Mingary Creek 134, 148–150, 152
Moller, G 26
Moody, Ken vi, 186, 189
Moore, Douglas 181
Moroney, Peter vi, 115
Morse Code 178
Mosquito Creek 148. See Also Mingary

Creek
Motor Inspection Car (MIC) 6, 117
Mount Grainger 35
Mulyungarie Pastoral Station 174, 190
Mundi Mundi Pastoral Station 155
Munro, Trixie 76, 117–118
Murder 22, 131
Murphy, Joe 127
Murray, Percy 173
Mutooroo 17, 136, 143, 147–149, 154–155, 174, 190
   Height Above Sea Level 147
   Naming of 147
   Railway Station 148
   Railway Yard 148–149, 151–152
Mutooroo Pastoral Station 155, 178, 190

N

Nackara 17, 35–36, 41–43, 45–49, 52, 54–61, 64, 66, 74, 104, 137
   Height Above Sea Level 47
   Naming of 47
   Railway Yard 48–50, 54, 56
Nantabibbie 17, 32–33, 35–36, 40, 42–45, 51, 55, 133, 154, 171
   174-mile Cutting 41, 43–44
   Height Above Sea Level 40
   Naming of 40
   Railway Station 40–41
   Railway Yard 41, 44
      Siding 40–41
Narrow Gauge ii, 1–3, 12, 16, 21, 29, 37, 43, 56, 63, 93, 101, 114, 130, 137, 162, 167, 185
Nelson, Herb 38–39
New South Wales vi, 1–2, 12, 35, 62, 122, 140, 142, 155, 162–163, 178–179
Noble, Jeff iii, vi
Noble, Lionel ix, 50, 85, 107, 136, 166, 193
Noble, Lorace vi, 105
Noble, Mark iii–iv, vi, 28
Noble, Meryn iv, 118
Norman, Bruce 189
Norman, Kevin 188
Norman, Snow 188
Northern Territory 3

O

O'Brien, Ian 73
O'Callaghan, Jack 178
O'Connell, Mrs 124
O'Dea, Chris vi
O'Dea, Jack vi, 145–146
O'Riley, Frank 114
Olary 15, 17, 102, 108, 111–116, 119, 121–122, 125–127, 141, 147, 157, 188–189
   Height Above Sea Level 111, 121
   Naming of 111
   Railway Station 110
   Railway Yard 110, 112, 114, 116, 118–119
   Reservoir 116
Olary Creek 102, 113–114, 122, 125
Olsen, Mervyn 10
Oodla Wirra 14, 17, 22–23, 27–28, 30–36, 38–40, 43, 66
   Flux Mine 35
   Height Above Sea Level 27
   Naming of 27
   Railway Station 26, 30–32
   Railway Yard 27, 30, 35–38
      Loco Depot 36
      Siding 32, 38
   Reservoir 36
   Stationmaster 26
Ore Concentrate 1–3, 12, 35, 135
Ore Train 13, 16, 56, 84, 131, 143
Oulnina 17, 89–93, 96–99
   Height Above Sea Level 89
   Naming of 89
   Railway Station 88, 90
   Railway Yard 89, 91
Outalpa 17, 96–97, 102, 107–108, 111–114, 116–117, 141, 156
   Gold Mine 106
   Height Above Sea Level 102
   Naming of 102
   Railway Station 103
   Railway Yard 102, 107
   Sand Cutting 104–105
Overalls 51
Overhead Tank 5–6, 22–23, 26, 28–29, 36, 46, 61, 74, 106, 132, 158, 163, 165

P

Paper Train 16–17, 23, 168
Paratoo 17, 50, 55, 60–61, 64–66, 68–71, 74–75, 117
   Height Above Sea Level 60
   Railway Station 61–62, 64–65

Railway Yard 65–68
Reservoir 61
Signal Cabin 62–63, 66
Paratoo Pastoral Station 66, 68, 70
Parliament of South Australia 1–2
Parnaroo 32, 41
Passenger Trains 5–6, 16, 23, 49, 94, 116, 130, 137, 143, 156, 161–163, 173
Patterson, Jim 169–170
Peecharra 42, 44–45, 47–48, 51–52, 55–56
  Height Above Sea Level 45, 47
  Railway Station 45
  Railway Yard 43, 45
    Siding 45–46
  Reservoir 46
Persil Washing Powder 51
Peterborough iii, vii, 3, 5, 8, 10–15, 17–23, 27–28, 30, 32, 37, 40, 44–45, 47, 50–51, 53, 55–58, 60, 65, 68, 72, 77–79, 83–84, 89, 93, 98–100, 102, 105–107, 111, 113, 117–119, 121, 128, 130, 132–133, 137–138, 140–142, 145, 147, 152, 154, 156, 163, 165, 173, 183, 185, 188, 191
  Bell Cabin 4–5
  Hurlstone Street iii, 6–7
  Loco Depot 5–10, 36, 153
    Gantry 7–9
    Loco Pit 5–6, 9
    Roundhouse 5, 8–9, 153
    Turntable 5–6, 8–9, 17, 153
  Main Street 8
  Peterborough Hotel 5
  Porter, Crossing Keeper 6–7
  Railway Hotel 5, 8, 120
  Railway Picnic 10–11, 22–23, 94
  Railway Station 4–5, 10, 23, 115
  Railway Terrace 5–6, 117
  Railway Yard iv, 3–7, 9–10, 13, 17, 171
  Silver Street 6
  Yankee Dip 18–20
  Yardmaster 4–5, 7, 9
Peterborough Division iii, v, 2, 12, 19, 74, 85, 114, 124–125, 131, 137, 190–192
Peters, Bill 181
Petersburg 1–2, 35. See Also Peterborough
Petropolous, Harry 22
Piano 34, 187
Pilot Crew 152

Pine Creek 90, 154–156
Pine Creek Pastoral Station 190
Place, Bill 189
Plane. See Aeroplane
Plummer Villa 110
Pocket Watch, Railway 50, 59
Pocketknife 145
Police 10, 70, 109, 170, 189
Polson 183
Port Augusta 1
Port Lincoln 10, 188
Port Pirie 1–3, 5, 10, 12–13, 35, 130, 189, 192
  Smelter 3, 12, 109
Porter, Railway 30, 40, 48, 76, 82, 90, 115, 118–119, 178, 186, 191
Post Master General 178
Post Office 49, 74, 141, 163, 183
Postler, Kurt 38
Pranks. See Comradeship
Produce Train 16, 82, 127
Pump 21, 23, 26, 28–29, 61, 66, 69, 132, 165

Q

Queensland 173, 191
Quorn 1, 3, 5, 66, 98, 138, 192

R

Rabbits 61, 71, 99, 107
Radio 125, 175
Radium Hill 104, 129–130, 132, 142, 188–189
Rasmus, Les vi, 21, 23, 26, 29
Rawlins, Harcourt 30
Rawlins, M 31
Redex Trial 156
Reece, Tom 106
Reed, E 181
Refreshment Rooms 17, 94–95, 163
Reservoir 44, 69
Reynolds, JJ 99
Richardson, G 117
Rifle 131, 146, 179, 186
Ritchie, Jim vi, 137, 139
Roads, Ross 188
Robb, Ross 135, 164
Rosterman 188
Rowse, Mel 10–11, 51
Royal Australian Navy 84

Rutherford, Alf 189
Rutherford, Brian 189
Ryan, Charlie 53
Ryan, Laurie 188

S

Saint, Ken 86
Saltbush 133, 147
Sandalwood 70, 74
Schell, Ray vi, 10–11, 164
School 15, 27, 49, 158, 163, 182–183, 186, 191
Schurmann, Pastor 72
Scorpions 144
Scotch Block. See Derailment
Shanahan, Jack 171
Shea, Martin 182
Shearers 183
Sheehan, Barney 30
Sheep 41, 46, 61, 66, 68, 70–71, 74–75, 79, 102, 105, 133, 147–148, 173–174, 189–190
Sheerlock, Andrew 179, 181
Sheerlock, Bessie 183
Sheerlock, George 181
Sheerlock, Jack 181
Sheerlock, Laurie 181
Sheerlock, Mary 180, 184
Sheerlock, William 174, 177
Shermer, Fay (nee Finlay) vi
Shift Work 3, 9–10, 15, 25, 51, 99, 105, 168–169, 173, 187
Shovel/Shovelling 18, 25, 51–52, 58, 64, 66, 75, 80–82, 114, 120, 125, 160–161
  Measuring Up 51
Shunting 7–9, 13, 41, 44, 56, 62, 65–66, 118, 127, 137, 144, 162, 171, 173, 186
Signalling 5, 7, 22, 24, 27, 30, 33, 38, 41, 48, 58, 60, 62–63, 65–66, 75, 79, 81, 88, 91, 93, 99–101, 103, 116, 144, 173, 191
  Signal, Starting 58, 62, 65
Signalman 19, 24, 33, 46, 48, 54, 58, 60, 62, 65–66, 91, 96, 104, 107, 136, 141, 191
Silver 1–2, 44
Silverton 1, 102, 109, 141
Silverton Tramway 2, 12, 162, 178–179, 188, 190–191
Sleep, Cliff 'Nugget' 90, 92, 141
Sleep, Ken vi, 53, 66, 105, 113, 160

Sleepers 34, 69, 76, 114, 130, 137, 152, 165
Slush Lamp 142
Smallacombe, Peter vi
Smith, Andrew 155
Smith, Jim 181
Smith, Mrs Eileen (nee Sheerlock) vi, 142, 174–183
Smith, Rodney 49
Smith, Sir Keith 155
Smith, Sir Ross 155
Snails, White 35
Snake 66–67, 90, 108, 156, 166
Snow, Jim 189
South Australian Railways ii–iii, v, 2–3, 12, 19, 72, 111, 133, 137–138, 164, 190
SP Bookmaker 189
Spencer Gulf 12
Spielers Creek 154
Standard Gauge 12, 28, 34, 107, 110, 113–114, 125, 130, 140
Standardisation 110–111, 135, 192
Stationmaster 186
Stewart, Nellie 180
Stock 30, 49, 64, 74, 79, 97–98, 105, 162, 173, 179, 186
Stock Train 16, 77, 98, 123, 162
Storeroom 51
Summerton, Lionel 107
Sunnybrae 18
Swagman 56, 108–109
  Jump the Rattler 108
Swanston, Harry 181
Swanston, Tom 164

T

Talbot, HC 72
Tattawuppa Hill 55
Teague, Jack 42
Telephone 40, 60, 96, 100, 104–106, 120–121, 168, 170
Television 96
Tennis 28, 49, 117, 142, 171, 179, 187
Terowie 1, 3, 5, 13, 21, 30, 102, 128, 192
Teske, Guenter 37
Thackaringa Pastoral Station 190
Thevenard 186
Thomas, 'Sparks' 137
Thomas, Graham 39
Thompson, F 181
Three Mile Creek 143, 149

Thunderstorm 112, 137, 140, 152
   Rainfall 38, 137, 151, 157
Thyer, James 18
Tietz 49
Timetable 17
Tindale, Professor NB 72
Town Hall 5, 10
Train Control/Controller 20, 48, 55, 60, 92, 106–107, 127, 151, 156, 171
Train Order 40, 126, 143
Traveller's Rest 30
Triangles, Railway 17, 61, 64
Trike, Railway 107, 148
Tucker Box 15, 81, 119, 153, 167
Tucker Train 16, 69, 96, 118, 140, 143–144
Twigden, Max 78, 86, 108, 113

U

Ucolta iii, 13–14, 18, 22–24, 30
   Amelia Park 23
   Dowd's Hill Tunnel 14, 18, 20–22, 24
   Height Above Sea Level 18
   Naming of 18
   Railway Reservoir 21, 23
   Railway Station 17, 28
   Railway Yard 22–27
      Siding 23

V

Victoria 10
Victory, Austin 9
Viney, Harry 69

W

Wakefield Street Hospital 132
Walloway 67
Walsh, Tom 24
Ward, C 181
Warrawarumbie Creek 80, 82, 90
Washaway 107, 112–113, 150, 152
Wastell, Alan 190
Water Column 6, 17, 22, 24, 38–40, 61, 66, 77, 116, 141, 144
Water Tanks 29, 36–38, 66–67, 99
Waters, Arnold 181
Waters, Ethel 180
Watson, Ralph 36
Wattle Tree 44, 133
Waukaringa 69, 75
Wawirra 100–102, 104
   Height Above Sea Level 100
   Naming of 100
Wawirra Creek 102
Wawirra Pastoral Station 102
Weekly, Bob 188
Weich, Heine vi
Well (water) 6, 26, 28–29, 98–99, 111
Well Paddock Creek 90
Welsby, Alan vi, 131–132
Western Endeavour Historical Train 81, 138
Westinghouse Air Brake 38
Wheat 23–24, 29, 49–50, 81, 186
White, Ted 188
Whitford, Tom 99
Wight, George 'Gonga' vi, 118–119
Williams, Archie vi, 14, 24, 77–78, 106
Wills, John 86
Wind 105, 123, 149, 173
Windmill 29, 61
Winkworth, King 84, 86
Winnininnie 17, 74, 79–81, 86, 89–90
   Height Above Sea Level 79
   Naming of 79
   Railway Station 85
Winnininnie Pastoral Station 79
Witting, WH 154
Wondai 191
Woodall, Joe 115
Woods, Cecil 26
Woods, Charlie 26
Woods, Olive 182
Woodville 57
Wool 41, 50, 74, 147, 184, 190
Woolcock, Fred 26
World War II 3, 37, 84, 119, 131, 171, 191–192

X

X-class Vehicles 35

Y

Y for George 146
Yates, Merv vi, 163
YMCA 5, 57, 120
Youngman, Norman 144
Yugoslav 186
Yunta 17, 34, 55, 70, 72, 74–77, 79, 81–84, 89–90
   Height Above Sea Level 74

    Naming of 72
    Railway Station 73, 76, 84
    Railway Yard 74-75, 77-78, 84
    Stationmaster 73-74
Yunta Creek 74, 79, 82

Z
Z-class Vehicles 74
Zilm, Oscar 115
Zinc Corporation 178

www.ingramcontent.com/pod-product-compliance
Lightning Source LLC
Chambersburg PA
CBHW072001070526
44583CB00015B/1282